Germany Tour Guide 2025

GW01314713

Discover the Heart of Europe| Unveiling Germany's Hidden Gems and Cultural Marvels in this Ultimate Travel Guide!

Katarina Weiss

© Copyright 2025 - All rights reserved.

The contents of this book may not be reproduced, duplicated, or transmitted without the direct written permission of the author or publisher.

Under no circumstances will the publisher or author be held liable for any damages, recovery, or financial loss due to the information contained in this book. Neither directly nor indirectly.

Legal Notice:

This book is protected by copyright. This book is for personal use only. You may not modify, distribute, sell, use, quote, or paraphrase any part or content of this book without the permission of the author or publisher.

Disclaimer Notice:

Please note that the information contained in this document is for educational and entertainment purposes only. Every effort has been made to present accurate, current, reliable, and complete information. No warranties of any kind are stated or implied. The reader acknowledges that the author is not offering legal, financial, medical, or professional advice. The contents of this book have been taken from various sources. Please consult a licensed professional before attempting any of the techniques described in this book.

By reading this document, the reader agrees that under no circumstances will the author be liable for any direct or indirect loss arising from the use of the information contained in this document, including but not limited to - errors, omissions, or inaccuracies.

Table of Contents

Introduction 3
Chapter 1: Travel Essentials 5
Chapter 2: Must Visit Places in Germany 22
Chapter 3: Itineraries 83
Chapter 4: Best Restaurants and Cuisine 89
Chapter 5: Accommodations in Germany 94
Chapter 6: Cultural Activities in Germany 99
Chapter 7: Nightlife And Festivals In Germany 102
Chapter 8: Souvenirs And Shopping in Germany 110
Chapter 9: Tips For Traveling in Germany 116
Conclusion 120

Introduction

Welcome to a place of fascinating contrasts, where elegant modern architecture blends with old castles and where traditional beer gardens coexist with cutting-edge art galleries. Enter the heart of Europe and set out on a breathtaking journey through Germany's varied landscapes and energetic cities.

Germany is one of the most alluring locations on the continent because of its fascinating history, vibrant culture, and spectacular natural beauty. Every nook of this magical country holds a narrative waiting to be found, from the charming fairytale villages of Bavaria to the busy metropolis of Berlin.

Start your journey by becoming lost in the fascinating fusion of old and new. Discover the famous city of Berlin, where the Berlin Wall's relics serve as somber witnesses to a divided history. Discover the city's vibrant creative energy by exploring its innumerable galleries, top-notch museums, and hip neighborhoods like Kreuzberg and Friedrichshain.

When you venture outside of the city, Germany's picturesque beauty will be revealed to you. With its mysterious attraction, the Black Forest draws you into its depths with twisting trails and emerald-green scenery. The majestic peaks of the Bavarian Alps kiss the sky, beckoning hikers and nature lovers to take in their breathtaking splendor.

However, Germany's appeal extends beyond its natural beauty. Enjoy a symphony of flavors as you indulge in the cuisine of the nation. Germany's cuisine is as diverse as its regions, ranging from robust sausages and pretzels to delicious pastries and world-famous beers.

Immerse yourself in Germany's rich traditions, where colorful festivals and celebrations bring folklore and centuries-old practices to life. Enjoy the ethereal allure of the Christmas markets, where the aroma of mulled wine and gingerbread fills the air. Watch as locals and tourists congregate in Munich to lift their steins in unison in celebration of Oktoberfest.

Germany has a wealth of experiences that will make a lasting impression on your soul, whether you are looking for history, adventure, or just a chance to relax in a lovely setting. So put on your hiking boots, grab your camera, and let Germany's allure lead you on an adventure you will not soon forget.

Prepare to be enchanted by the enchanting scenery, energetic cities, and friendly people of Germany. Your journey is waiting. Begin here by reviewing what all Germany has to offer, getting some thoughts as to where you want to go, and then booking your trip. To see all Germany has to offer, you need months. Most of us have nowhere near that, so plan carefully, do your research, which we hope to help with herein, and take full advantage of your time in Germany.

Chapter 1: Travel Essentials

Best time to visit.

The best time to travel to Germany depends on your preferences and what you want to experience during your trip. Germany has a temperate seasonal climate, and each season offers unique attractions and activities. Here's a breakdown of the different seasons:

1. Spring (March to May):

   - Mild temperatures: Spring in Germany brings pleasant weather with temperatures gradually warming up. It's a great time to enjoy outdoor activities without the scorching heat of summer or the chilly cold of winter.

   - Blooming landscapes: The countryside bursts into life with colorful flowers and blossoming trees. Parks, gardens, and the famous cherry blossom trees in Bonn and Hamburg create picturesque settings for leisurely strolls and picnics.

   - Easter celebrations: Easter is an important holiday in Germany, and you can witness various cultural traditions like Easter egg hunts, bonfires, and markets selling Easter crafts and decorations.

   - Lower tourist crowds: Compared to the summer months, spring sees fewer tourists, allowing you to explore popular cities and attractions with relatively fewer crowds.

2. Summer (June to August):

- Warm weather: Summer in Germany brings warmer temperatures, making it ideal for outdoor activities and exploring the numerous lakes, rivers, and beaches across the country.

- Festivals and events: Summer is the festival season, including music festivals, open-air concerts, and cultural events. Major cities, including Berlin, Hamburg, Munich, and most others, host a range of events, offering a vibrant and lively atmosphere.

- Beer gardens and outdoor dining: German beer gardens come alive in the summer, providing a fantastic opportunity to sample local brews and traditional cuisine while enjoying the pleasant weather.

- Longer daylight hours: Summer days are longer, giving you more time to explore and enjoy the sights and attractions.

3. Autumn (September to November):

- Mild temperatures and fall foliage: Autumn in Germany is characterized by mild temperatures and stunning landscapes as trees change colors. The vibrant foliage provides a beautiful backdrop for hiking, cycling, and scenic drives through the countryside.

- Wine festivals: September is the beginning of wine harvest season, and various wine festivals take place in the wine regions, such as the Moselle Valley and the Rheingau. It's a great time to indulge in wine tastings and vineyard tours.

- Oktoberfest: The world-famous Oktoberfest in Munich usually starts in late September and spills over into early

October. It's a massive celebration of Bavarian culture featuring beer tents, traditional food, parades, and amusement rides.

- Lower tourist crowds: Compared to the summer, tourist numbers decline in autumn, allowing for a more relaxed and immersive experience.

4. Winter (December to February):

- Christmas markets: Germany is renowned for its enchanting Christmas markets, which offer a magical atmosphere with twinkling lights, festive decorations, and delicious seasonal treats. Cities like Nuremberg, Dresden, and Cologne have some of the most famous markets…and the most crowded. 2024 saw record crowds in many places, and more to come in 2025. Try some lesser-known destinations, like Aachen, Heidelburg or Koblenz

- Winter sports: If you enjoy winter sports like skiing, snowboarding, or ice skating, Germany's Bavarian Alps provide excellent opportunities. Resorts like Garmisch-Partenkirchen and Oberstdorf offer a range of winter activities.

- Carnival season: In February, Germany celebrates the carnival season with colorful parades, costumes, and street parties. Cologne and Düsseldorf are known for their lively carnival celebrations.

- Lower tourist crowds (except during Christmas markets): With the exception of the popular Christmas market period, winter generally sees fewer tourists, making it a good time to explore attractions and museums with fewer crowds.

What to pack

When packing for a trip to Germany, it's essential to consider the time of year and the activities you plan to engage in. However, here is a general list of items you should consider packing:

1. Clothing:

   - Comfortable walking shoes

   - Lightweight, breathable clothing for summer or warmer months

   - Layered clothing for cooler seasons

- Rain jacket or umbrella
- Hat or cap for sun protection
- Swimsuit (if visiting during summer or planning to visit lakes or spas)

2. Travel Documents:

    - Valid passport
    - Travel visa (if required)
    - Printed copies of hotel reservations, flight tickets, and other essential documents
    - Travel insurance information

3. Electronics:

    - Universal power adapter (Germany uses Type C and F sockets)
    - Mobile phone and charger

- Camera and extra memory cards

- Portable charger/power bank

- Most importantly, your cell phone with a plan that works overseas or a European SIM card. Everything is electronic these days, so for payment (think Apple Pay) or getting around (Google Maps), this is a 110% must!

4. Medications and Personal Items:

- Prescription medications (ensure they are properly labeled and carry a copy of the prescription)

- Over-the-counter medications (pain relievers, allergy medication, etc.)

- Toiletries (toothbrush, toothpaste, shampoo, etc.)

- Personal hygiene products

5. Miscellaneous:

- Money and credit/debit cards

- Guidebooks or maps

- Language phrasebook or translation app

- Travel-sized laundry detergent (if you plan to do laundry)

- Reusable water bottle

- Travel locks for securing luggage

- Daypack or tote bag for carrying essentials during outings

How to get there and move around

To get to Germany and move around within the country, you can follow these general steps:

1. **Travel to Germany**: Depending on where you are located, you can choose different modes of transportation to reach Germany. The most common options are:

    - **By air**: Book a flight to one of Germany's major airports, such as Frankfurt Airport, Munich Airport, or Berlin Brandenburg Airport. Many international airlines offer direct flights to Germany from various locations around the world.

    - **By train**: If you are in a neighboring country with a railway connection to Germany, you can consider taking a train. Germany has an extensive rail network, and there are often convenient connections from neighboring European countries.

- **By bus**: Long-distance buses are another option, particularly if you are in a nearby country. Several bus companies operate routes to Germany, providing affordable travel options.

- **By car**: If you have your own vehicle or prefer driving, you can enter Germany by road. Ensure you are familiar with the driving regulations, have the necessary documentation (such as an international driver's license), and consider any border crossing requirements.

2. **Entry requirements**: Before traveling to Germany, it's essential to check the entry requirements based on your nationality. Make sure you have a valid passport with sufficient validity and any necessary visas or travel documents required for entry into Germany. It's essential to comply with the specific entry regulations and have all the required paperwork in order.

3. **Transportation within Germany**: Once you arrive in Germany, you have several options for moving around within the country:

- **Trains**: Germany's national railway operator, Deutsche Bahn, operates an extensive train network. You can use regional trains, intercity trains, or high-speed trains to travel between cities and regions within Germany. Train travel is generally efficient and offers good connectivity.

- **Buses**: Long-distance buses are a popular and affordable mode of transportation in Germany. Companies like FlixBus and MeinFernbus operate routes between cities and towns across the country. Local buses are also available within cities and towns, serving as a convenient option for short distances.

- **Trams and U-Bahn/S-Bahn**: Many major German cities have tram systems and metro networks known as U-Bahn (subway) or S-Bahn (urban rail). These systems provide efficient and convenient transportation within the cities, connecting different neighborhoods and attractions.

- **Taxis**: Taxis can be found in most German cities. You can either hail them on the street or locate taxi stands. Taxis are a more expensive option compared to public transportation but offer door-to-door convenience.

- **Car rentals**: If you prefer the flexibility of driving, you can rent a car from various car rental companies available at airports and in cities. Germany has a well-maintained network of highways (Autobahn) that allows for convenient travel between cities and regions.

4. **Public transportation tickets**: In Germany, you usually need a ticket to use public transportation. You can purchase single tickets or day passes from ticket machines or counters at train stations, tram stops, or bus stations for local transportation within cities. Some cities also offer transport cards or

rechargeable tickets for multiple trips, which can be more cost-effective if you plan to use public transportation frequently.

5. **Navigation and maps**: To navigate within Germany, you can use various navigation apps or websites such as Google Maps or local German apps. These tools help you plan routes, find the nearest public transportation stops, and provide real-time information about schedules, delays, and alternative routes. They can be valuable resources for getting around efficiently. As before, our recommendation is the use of your in-phone map app.

Practical information for visitors.

Language and communication

As a visitor to Germany, I find it helpful to have some information about the language and communication in the country. Here are a few key points to keep in mind:

- Official Language: German is the official language of Germany. Most Germans speak it as their first language, and it is the language used for official purposes, government, education, and the media.

- English Proficiency: In major cities and tourist areas, you can generally find people who speak English, especially among the younger population and those working in the tourism industry. However, it's always a good idea to learn some basic German phrases to help you navigate everyday situations.

- Greetings: Common greetings in German include "Guten Tag" (Good day) for formal situations or during the day, "Guten Morgen" (Good morning) until around noon, and "Guten Abend" (Good evening) in the late afternoon or evening. Handshakes are a typical form of greeting, but friends may also hug or kiss each other on the cheek.

- Politeness: Germans value politeness and respect in their interactions. It's customary to use "Bitte" (please) and "Danke" (thank you) frequently. When entering a shop or restaurant, it's common to greet the staff with a friendly "Guten Tag" and say "Auf Wiedersehen" (goodbye) when leaving.

- Language Barrier: If you encounter difficulties communicating due to language barriers, don't be afraid to use basic English phrases, gestures, or even a translation app to help convey your message. Many Germans will appreciate your efforts to communicate and will try to assist you.

- Public Transportation: If you plan to use public transportation, such as buses, trains, or trams, it's beneficial to learn some basic German terms like "Fahrkarte" (ticket), "Bahnhof" (train station), "Bushaltestelle" (bus stop), and "Ausstieg" (exit). Most transportation systems have signs and announcements in both German and English.

- Emergency Situations: In case of an emergency, dial 112 to reach the emergency services (police, fire brigade, or ambulance). You can say "Notfall" (emergency) to seek immediate assistance.

Here are some common German phrases that can be useful for a visitor in Germany:

- Guten Tag / Hallo - Good day / Hello

- Wie geht es Ihnen? - How are you?

- Sprechen Sie Englisch? - Do you speak English?

- Ja - Yes

- Nein - No

- Danke - Thank you

- Bitte - Please/You're welcome

- Entschuldigung - Excuse me

- Ich verstehe nicht - I don't understand

- Wo ist...? - Where is...?

- Wie viel kostet das? - How much does that cost?

- Haben Sie Empfehlungen? - Do you have any recommendations?

- Ich hätte gerne... - I would like...

- Kann ich mit Kreditkarte zahlen? - Can I pay with a credit card?

- Wo ist die Toilette? - Where is the restroom?

- Guten Appetit - Enjoy your meal

- Prost - Cheers

- Auf Wiedersehen / Tschüss - Goodbye

Currency and banking

The official currency of Germany is the Euro (€). Here is some general information about currency and banking for visitors in Germany:

- Currency Exchange: You can exchange your currency to Euros at banks, currency exchange offices, or some hotels. Banks usually offer competitive exchange rates. It's advisable to compare rates and fees before making an exchange.

- ATMs: Germany has a widespread network of ATMs, known as "Geldautomaten" or "Bankautomaten," where you can withdraw Euros using your debit or credit card. Look for ATMs affiliated with major networks such as Visa, Mastercard, or Maestro. Inform your bank about your travel plans to ensure your card works internationally.

- Credit and Debit Cards: Credit and debit cards are widely accepted in Germany, especially in larger cities and tourist areas.

Visa and Mastercard are the most commonly accepted cards, followed by Maestro and American Express. However, carrying some cash for smaller establishments or places that may not accept cards is always a good idea.

- Banking Hours: Most banks in Germany are open from Monday to Friday between 9:00 AM and 4:00 PM. Some banks may close earlier on Fridays. ATMs, on the other hand, are available 24/7 and can be used for various banking services.

- Identification and Security: When conducting banking transactions in Germany, it's advisable to carry a valid form of identification, such as a passport. Additionally, be cautious when using ATMs and ensure the machine is in a secure location to minimize the risk of card skimming or other fraudulent activities.

- Currency Restrictions: There are no restrictions on the amount of foreign currency you can bring into or take out of Germany. However, if you are carrying 10,000 Euros or more (or the equivalent in another currency), you must declare it at customs upon arrival or departure.

Safety information

As a visitor in Germany, it's important to be aware of certain safety information to ensure a pleasant and secure experience. Here are some safety tips:

- Emergency Numbers: Familiarize yourself with the emergency contact numbers in Germany. The general emergency number is 112 for all kinds of emergencies. If you need to reach the police, call 110.

- Health and Travel Insurance: Before traveling to Germany, ensure you have comprehensive health insurance that covers any medical emergencies or accidents. Carry your insurance documents with you at all times.

- Personal Safety: Germany is generally considered a safe country, but it's still important to take precautions. Keep an eye on your belongings, especially in crowded tourist areas, and be cautious of pickpockets. Avoid displaying expensive items or large amounts of cash in public.

- Public Transportation: Germany has an extensive and efficient public transportation system. When using buses, trains, or trams, be mindful of your personal belongings and stay vigilant. Avoid traveling alone late at night, particularly in less crowded areas.

- Road Safety: If you plan on driving in Germany, familiarize yourself with local traffic rules and signage. Always wear seatbelts, and ensure all passengers are appropriately restrained. Follow speed limits, and be cautious of pedestrians and cyclists.

- Scams and Fraud: Be cautious of scams targeting tourists. Be skeptical of anyone approaching you with unsolicited offers, and be mindful when sharing personal or financial information.

Only use reputable services for currency exchange or ticket purchases.

- Natural Hazards: Germany is not prone to major natural disasters, but it's important to stay informed about any potential risks during your visit. Pay attention to weather forecasts and follow instructions from local authorities in case of severe weather conditions.

- Health and Safety Regulations: Follow health and safety guidelines, such as wearing face masks and practicing good hygiene, especially during times of public health concerns. Stay updated on any travel advisories or regulations related to the COVID-19 pandemic.

- Cultural Sensitivity: Respect local customs, traditions, and laws. Familiarize yourself with basic etiquette and cultural norms to avoid any unintentional offense or misunderstanding.

- Stay Informed: Stay updated on current events and any travel advisories or warnings issued by your home country's embassy or consulate in Germany. Register your travel details with your embassy for any emergency notifications.

Chapter 2: Must Visit Places in Germany

There is so much to see and do in Germany, but as to what is seen, that is relative, depending on the traveler and their specific tastes, which do tend to vary widely, even between a couple traveling together (!). In this section following, we have provided what we believe are the top city destinations in Germany, including a good list of things to see once there. Two of these cities, and a few more added at the end without explicit detail, are what I would consider to be Hidden Gems, in that most travelers to Germany do not make it to these, or are under the radar, or are under-appreciated

A quick note, too, on **Hidden Gems**. This, too, is a very subject term. For some, a hidden gem might be a gallery tucked away that few know about. For others, it could be the ruins of a castle that is hardly visited. Further, some of these gems may well be on the standard itinerary for some. I have tried providing a few different options and thoughts in most cities. However, if you are really looking for hidden gems, get the local experience on the ground, or for a higher level, take the time to check out the cities we show as true Hidden Gems.

Also, please note that visiting hours and charges may vary, so it is advisable to check the official websites or contact the attractions directly for the most up-to-date information. Or, take a look at your app; Google Maps does a great job of confirming times. Some museums are closed on Mondays.

Germany Travel Guide 2023

Berlin

Berlin, the capital of Germany, is a vibrant and seductive city that offers a unique combination of culture, tradition, and modernity.

Here are some of Berlin's most popular tourist attractions, along with details on how to get there, how much entrance costs, and what to see there:

- **Berlin Wall**

The Berlin Wall, which was in place between 1961 and 1989, divided Berlin. The German Democratic Republic (GDR), commonly known as East Germany, built it to prevent its citizens from emigrating to West Berlin, which was ruled by the Federal Republic of Germany (FRG), popularly known as West Germany.

Construction on the Berlin Wall began on August 13, 1961. Concrete barriers, barbed wire, and watchtowers around it. The wall completely encircled West Berlin and separated it from East Berlin and East Germany; its length was approximately 155 kilometers (96 miles).

The fundamental objective of the Berlin Wall was to stop the large-scale migration of East Germans to the more prosperous West Germany. Before the wall was constructed, over 2.5 million East Germans had fled to the West, which posed problems for the GDR's economy and politics. The wall physically represented the Iron Curtain that separated Western Europe from the Eastern Bloc during the Cold War.

When visiting the Berlin Wall, there are a number of significant tourist attractions you should consider seeing. Some of the top locations with ties to the Berlin Wall include the following:

- East Side Gallery: The East Side Gallery, a must-see site in Friedrichshain-Kreuzberg, is located along the Mühlenstraße. It is a section of the Berlin Wall that has colorful murals painted on it by artists from all over the world that act as an outdoor gallery. Concepts of liberty, harmony, and societal change are represented in the artwork.

- One of the most well-known border crossings between East and West Berlin during the Cold War was Checkpoint Charlie. With a reproduction of the guardhouse and a sign designating the ancient border crossing, it is now a well-liked tourist destination. The Checkpoint Charlie Museum, another attraction close by, features exhibits on the Berlin Wall's history and accounts of failed escapes.

- Berlin Wall Memorial and Documentation Center: This memorial site, which is situated on Bernauer Strasse, offers a thorough overview of the history of the Berlin Wall. It consists of an outdoor exhibit, a watchtower-equipped piece of the wall that has been restored, and an underground visitor center with educational displays, pictures, and personal accounts.

- Gedenkstätte Berliner Mauer: This memorial, which is located close to the Nordbahnhof train station, protects a portion of the ancient border strip. It comprises an exhibition that details the history of the Berlin Wall and its effects on Berliners' lives while providing a view into the reality of the border fortifications.

- Topography of Terror: The Topography of Terror museum, close to Potsdamer Platz, features an extensive display on the Nazi dictatorship and the following construction of the Berlin Wall, despite not being specifically focused on the Berlin Wall. It offers a historical background and enlightens visitors on more significant historical occurrences related to the wall's construction.

- Mauerpark: The lively park in the Prenzlauer Berg neighborhood was formerly a section of the death strip. Today, it is a well-liked gathering spot with a flea market, karaoke shows, and a hill where people congregate for picnics and take in expansive city views.

- Visitor fees are not required, and the outdoor areas are open 24 hours a day.

Exploring these highlights, which provide a wide variety of experiences, you can learn more about the history, creativity, and relevance of the Berlin Wall. Don't forget to spend some time strolling along the wall's remains, which are scattered around the city and act as continual reminders of the city's divided past.

- **Museum Island (Museumsinsel)**

Berlin's Museumsinsel is a popular tourist destination and a UNESCO World Heritage site. It is situated on an island in the Spree River and houses a number of well-known museums. Some of Museum Island's leading tourist destinations are listed below:

- One of the most well-known museums on the island is the Pergamon Museum, which is renowned for its remarkable collection of antiquities. The Pergamon Altar, the Market Gate of Miletus, and the Ishtar Gate of Babylon are among the highlights.

- The Neues Museum is home to a sizable collection of ancient Egyptian and Paleolithic antiquities. Its most well-known feature is the bust of Nefertiti, one of the most famous pieces of ancient Egyptian art.

- Altes Museum: The oldest museum on Museum Island, the Altes Museum displays classical artifacts. It features a sizable collection of sculptures, vases, jewelry, and other works of Greek and Roman art.

- The Alte Nationalgalerie, often known as the Old National Gallery, specializes in works of art from the 19th century. The Romantic, Impressionist, and early Modernist periods are well represented in its magnificent collection of paintings and sculptures.

- The Bode Museum is renowned for its extensive collection of sculptures, Byzantine artwork, and coinage. It includes treasures like the Statue of Charlemagne and the Reformation and

Counter-Reformation exhibition, as well as works from the Middle Ages to the Eighteenth Century.

- Berliner Dom: Although the Berliner Dom (Berlin Cathedral) is not a museum in and of itself, it is well worth a visit because it is close to Museum Island. The beautiful, stunningly designed Protestant church has a dome that provides sweeping views.

- Spree River: Visitors can enjoy a picturesque backdrop thanks to Museum Island's location on the Spree River. To experience Berlin's ancient canals, you can take a leisurely stroll along the riverbanks or even go on a boat excursion.

- Visiting hours and charges vary by museum:

➢ Pergamon Museum: Daily 10 am to 6 pm (10 euros admission fee)

➢ Neues Museum: Daily 10 am to 6 pm (12 euros admission fee)

➢ Altes Museum: Daily 10 am to 6 pm (12 euros admission fee)

➢ Bode Museum: Daily 10 am to 6 pm (12 euros admission fee)

➢ Alte Nationalgalerie: Daily 10 am to 6 pm (10 euros admission fee)

These are just a few of the highlights you can explore on Museum Island. Each museum offers a unique experience, and art and history enthusiasts will find plenty to appreciate during their visit.

- **Reichstag Building**

A well-known landmark in Berlin, Germany, the Reichstag Building is renowned for both its historical importance and its exquisite architectural design. The Reichstag Building's tourist attractions include the following:

- Visit the Dome: The glass dome of the Reichstag Building, which provides sweeping vistas of Berlin, is the building's most well-known feature. The rooftop terrace of the dome, accessible via elevator, offers visitors stunning views of the cityscape, including famous sites like the Brandenburg Gate and the Tiergarten.

- Plenary Chamber: Though entrance to the Plenary Chamber is restricted, people may still see it through a glass pane from the inside of the dome at the Reichstag, which serves as the location of the German Parliament (Bundestag). The chamber serves as a reminder of the history and democracy of Germany.

- Historical Exhibits: The Reichstag Building is home to a number of historical displays that shed light on Germany's political past. The building's history is covered in the ongoing display "Wege, Irrwege, Umwege" (Paths, Dead Ends, Detours), which highlights the building's damage during World War II and subsequent reconstruction.

- Use the audio guide, which is available in several languages, as you tour the Reichstag Building. This detailed reference offers information about the building's history, architecture, and political system in Germany.

- Garden & Surroundings: A lovely garden area, which includes the Tiergarten park, surrounds the Reichstag Building. Visitors can take in the beauty of the structure and its surrounds while enjoying a leisurely stroll, having a picnic, or simply relaxing in nature.

- Light and Sound Show: The Reichstag Building is frequently illuminated with vibrant lights at night, producing a spellbinding visual display. The lighting scheme highlights the architectural details and heightens the structure's appeal.

- Daily from eight in the morning to midnight (admission times may vary) Costs: None (reservation required)

It's worth noting that due to security reasons and the popularity of the Reichstag Building as a tourist attraction, it's advisable to book your visit in advance through the official website of the German Bundestag. This ensures a smoother entry and enhances your overall experience.

- **Charlottenburg Palace**

The majestic palace complex known as Charlottenburg Palace may be found in Berlin, Germany's Charlottenburg neighborhood. When you visit Charlottenburg Palace, you can discover some of the following highlights:

- Palace Grounds: The Charlottenburg Gardens are a lovely set of gardens that surround the palace. Enjoy the well-kept grounds' well manicured lawns, attractive flowerbeds, and delightful paths by taking a leisurely stroll across them. A magnificent Orangery and a Belvedere tea house can also be found in the gardens.

- The Old Palace, also known as Alte Schloss, is the original part of Charlottenburg Palace. Admire the splendor of the Baroque and Rococo architecture as you explore its luxurious apartments. The spectacular Golden Gallery, the Porcelain Cabinet, and the Crown Prince's Apartments are only a few highlights.

- The 18th century saw the addition of the New Wing (Neuer Flügel) to the palace complex. The Porcelain Collection, which features a vast assortment of excellent Chinese and European porcelain, is housed there. Learn about the development of porcelain while admiring the fine craftsmanship.

- Mausoleum: Queen Louise's last resting place, which is next to the palace, is the Mausoleum. She was adored by the Prussian populace. Beautiful statues and an imposing marble sarcophagus can be found inside the mausoleum.

- The New Pavilion is a lovely building in the palace gardens, also known as the Little Palace (Kleines Schloss). Frederick the Great formerly spent his summers in this neoclassical pavilion. Explore the opulent rooms and take in the picturesque views from the terrace.

- Palace Chapel is a tiny yet lovely religious place that may be found in the Old Palace. Take time to see the gorgeous organ, stunning ceiling frescoes, and the detailed woodwork. The chapel is still used for religious services, and it also hosts concerts periodically.

- Palace Theatre: Located inside the palace complex, the Palace Theatre, also called the Court Theatre (Schlosstheater), is a venerable theater. It offers a glimpse into the performing arts of the eighteenth century. If possible, attend a performance or take a guided tour to appreciate the quaint setting and elaborate decor.

- Visiting hours: Tuesday to Sunday, 10 am to 6 pm. Charges: 12 euros (regular), additional fees for guided tours

The complex offers a rich cultural experience, allowing you to immerse yourself in the grandeur and history of Prussian royalty.

- **Potsdamer Platz**

Berlin, Germany's bustling and historic Potsdamer Platz, is the center of the city. It has experienced significant changes throughout time and is currently a thriving center of contemporary architecture, entertainment, commerce, and cultural activities. Here are a few Potsdamer Platz tourist attractions:

- Sony Center: This iconic glass and steel structure is a major landmark of Potsdamer Platz. It houses a variety of shops, restaurants, cinemas, and exhibition spaces. The futuristic design and the impressive roof make it a must-visit attraction.

- The Holocaust Memorial: Located just a short walk from Potsdamer Platz, the Memorial to the Murdered Jews of Europe, also known as the Holocaust Memorial, is a powerful and somber tribute to the victims of the Holocaust. The memorial consists of an array of concrete slabs of different heights, creating a thought-provoking and immersive experience.

- Daimler Contemporary: Art enthusiasts can visit the Daimler Contemporary, an art gallery showcasing contemporary works from renowned artists. The exhibition space focuses on modern and contemporary art, particularly emphasizing works related to mobility and technology.

- Potsdamer Platz Arkaden: If you're in the mood for some shopping, Potsdamer Platz Arkaden is a large shopping center with a wide range of stores, including popular international brands and boutiques. It's an excellent place to shop for fashion, accessories, electronics, and more.

- Berliner Philharmonie: Situated near Potsdamer Platz, the Berliner Philharmonie is home to the Berlin Philharmonic Orchestra. The concert hall is renowned for its exceptional acoustics and hosts a variety of classical music performances throughout the year. Be sure to check the schedule for any concerts or events during your visit.

- The Berlinale: Potsdamer Platz is one of the main venues for the Berlin International Film Festival, also known as the Berlinale. If you happen to visit during the festival, you can catch screenings of international films and red carpet events and experience the vibrant atmosphere of this prestigious event, which is not to be missed.

- Visiting hours: Open 24 hours. Charges: Free (some attractions may have separate admission fees.

- **Other Things to See in Berlin and Hidden Gems**

- **Brandenburg Gate** – Seen by many as the main landmark of the city, the Brandenburg Gate symbolizes reunification: Built in 1791, a large, magnificent square, the Parizer Platz, was established in front of the Gate, where famous buildings like the historic Hotel Adlon or the Academy of the Arts are located today.

- **Humboldt Forum**—Dedicated to human history, art, and culture, the Humboldt Forum includes two museums: the Ethnological Museum of Berlin and the Museum of Asian Art. The intriguing Friedrichswerder Church is nearby.
- Hidden Gems
    - **Computerspielmuseum** – If you love computer games, this museum is for you. Video games from 30-40 years ago up to today…and you can even play some of the games! Karl-Marx-Alee 93A
    - **Medieval City Walls** – Despite the wartime destruction of Berlin, some portions of the old city walls still remain. If

you want a glimpse of the history, stop by for a look. Waisenstrasse 2.

- o **Urban Nation** – A museum for urban contemporary art, this street art museum deviates from traditional artwork and a joy to take in. Bulowstrasse 7
- o **Spandau Citadel** – Dating back to the 12th century, this fort, more than a castle, is a well-preserved relic of Berlin from nearly a thousand years ago. It is a short way off the normal drag but easy to reach by public transport. Am Juliusturm 64

Hamburg

The second-largest city in Germany, Hamburg, is renowned for its dynamic culture, long maritime history, and beautiful architecture. In Hamburg, there are several tourist sites that provide a wide range of experiences. Here are a few of the main points:

- The world's largest warehouse district is located in **Speicherstadt**, a UNESCO World Heritage Site. Beautiful red-brick warehouses, canals, and bridges may be found here. In addition to housing attractions like **Miniatur Wunderland**, the biggest model railroad in the world, it is a well-liked location for photography.

- One of the most significant urban development initiatives in Europe is **HafenCity**, a contemporary waterfront neighborhood. Its outstanding modern buildings include the renowned Elbphilharmonie performance venue. Visitors can take in the expansive vistas from the Plaza, explore the International Maritime Museum, or embark on a boat cruise.

- Hamburg's entertainment quarter, **St. Pauli**, is well-known for its vibrant nightlife and the recognizable Reeperbahn. Bars, clubs, theaters, and places for adult entertainment fill this busy boulevard. It is a lively and exciting region that draws tourists from all around the world.

- **Miniatur Wunderland** is a must-see destination for people of all ages and is situated within Speicherstadt. It is the largest model railroad in the world and features painstakingly detailed tiny cities, landscapes, and railroads. The attention to detail and interactive features make it a fascinating experience.

- One of Hamburg's most well-known landmarks is **St. Michael's Church**, also known as "Michel" by locals. Visitors can ascend the church's tower for incredible views of the city.

The church's interior is also amazing, with lovely architecture and an elaborate organ.

- **Planten un Blomen**: In the center of Hamburg, this vast park provides a tranquil haven from the busy city. It has vibrant gardens, peaceful water features, and in the winter, even an ice rink. The park is a great area to take a leisurely stroll, have a picnic, or go to outdoor performances in the summer.

- **Hamburg Harbor**: As a prominent port city, Hamburg's harbor draws many visitors. Visitors can take boat cruises to see the bustling nautical industry, explore the harbor, and view the enormous container ships. Additionally, there are restaurants, museums, including the International Maritime Museum, and, on Sundays, the Hamburg Fish Market in the waterfront area.

- **The Hamburg Rathaus**, often known as City Hall, is a magnificent neo-renaissance structure situated in the heart of the city. It is a notable landmark due to its impressive architecture, elaborate interiors, and lovely courtyard. To learn about the history and government of the city, visitors can take guided tours.

- One of Germany's most prominent art museums, the **Kunsthalle Hamburg,** is a must-see for art lovers. It contains a sizable collection of European artwork by prominent artists that spans decades. The museum also offers a variety of art experiences through temporary exhibitions.

- The **Inner Alster and Outer Alster** are two calm bodies of water that make up the Alster Lakes, which are situated in the heart of the city. Visitors can rent paddleboats or go on boat cruises to explore the lakes. The nearby promenades provide beautiful scenery, eateries, and leisure activities.

- Hidden Gem—Park Fiction is a well-loved local park area overlooking the harbor. It is somewhat of a demonstration in ways against city development. It is a great place to come and view the harbor, sit back and enjoy the quirkiness of the "park."

- Hidden Gem—St. Nicholas Church was once considered the tallest building in the world. Now, its tower still stands as a monument and testament.

Munich

Munich, the capital of the German state of Bavaria, is well known for its rich past, beautiful architecture, and vibrant culture. The top tourist attractions in Munich are listed below, together with details on admission costs, hours of operation, and highlights:

- Munich's **Marienplatz** is the city's focal point and its beating heart. Historic structures surround it, and the New Town Hall, with its renowned glockenspiel, is a prominent landmark. The Glockenspiel plays twice a day at 11 am and 12 pm, and entrance to the square is free.

- **Nymphenburg Palace**: Just beyond the city's heart lies the exquisite Baroque palace known as **Nymphenburg Palace**. It was the summer home of the Bavarian kings and is surrounded by lovely gardens. The entrance price to the palace varies based on the regions you desire to visit. The large park and gardens, the **Marstallmuseum** (vehicle museum), and the grand royal halls are among of the highlights.

- Even bigger than Central Park in New York City, the **Englischer Garten** is one of the biggest urban parks on the planet. It offers tranquil surroundings, winding paths, and a lovely lake. Visitors can go on bike excursions, have picnics, or simply unwind in one of the classic beer gardens. Entrance is free.

- The former royal residence of the Wittelsbach kings is the **Munich Residenz**. It is a masterwork of architecture, displaying numerous architectural styles, from Renaissance to Neoclassical. Depending on the places you choose to visit, such as the royal apartments, the treasury, and the **Cuvilliés Theatre**, the palace offers various ticket choices.

- Car aficionados will appreciate a visit to the **BMW Welt & Museum**. The BMW Museum presents the company's history, and BMW Welt is a futuristic exhibition center where you can experience the brand's most recent inventions. There are guided tours available, and the entrance charge varies based on the package you select.

- **The Dachau Concentration Camp Memorial Site** is a solemn but significant destination that can be found just outside of Munich. It aims to bring to memory the horrors performed during the Nazi government. The memorial site offers free admission as well as guided excursions.

- One of the biggest scientific and technology museums in the world is the **Deutsches Museum**. It provides a wide range of displays addressing many scientific fields. You must pay to enter the museum, and you might easily spend hours examining its interesting exhibits and interactive displays.

- Hidden Gem. The **NS Dokumentationszentrum** is a bit of an under the radar museum that documents in great detail the rise of the Nazi party and the rather central role Munich had to play in these unfortunate events

- Hidden Gem. Schleissheim Palace is a beautiful palace somewhat off the beaten path but very well preserved and restored. It provides insight into how it looked during its grandest days. It is truly spectacular and a rare baroque garden complex.

Cologne

The vibrant and ancient city of Cologne, located in western Germany along the Rhine River, is renowned for its rich cultural heritage, stunning architecture, welcoming nature, and, of course, the Cathedral that overlooks the main bridge and the Rhine. Here are a handful of the main tourist attractions and landmarks in Cologne:

- The majestic Gothic masterpiece known as the **Cologne Cathedral** (Kölner Dom) is the most recognizable structure in the city and a UNESCO World Heritage site. The cathedral is a must-see destination because of its magnificent architecture, intricate stained glass windows, and breathtaking views from the top.

- **The Old Town (Altstadt)** of Cologne is a lovely neighborhood with winding cobblestone lanes, picturesque squares, and brightly painted homes. It has a great environment to explore and is home to many stores, cafes, and historic breweries.

- **Rhine River Promenade**: The picturesque Rhine River Promenade is a waterfront location ideal for leisurely strolls and taking in the river's breathtaking vistas. With its lovely cafes, restaurants, and gorgeous surroundings, it's a well-liked destination for both locals and tourists.

- **The Museum Ludwig** is a renowned art gallery that is close to the Cologne Cathedral and has an outstanding collection of modern and contemporary art. It features pieces by well-known painters like Warhol, Picasso, and Lichtenstein.

- **Hohenzollern Bridge**: The Hohenzollern Bridge, which spans the Rhine River, is well-known for its "love locks" in addition to being an important transit route. To represent their everlasting love, couples affix padlocks to the bridge and toss the key into the river.

- **The Chocolate Museum** (Schokoladenmuseum) provides a fascinating look at the development and history of this wonderful treat. Cologne is well recognized for its mouthwatering chocolates. The Botanical Gardens in Cologne are a tranquil oasis with stunning landscapes, greenhouses, and a broad variety of plant species. Visitors may learn about chocolate-making processes, indulge in tastings, and even manufacture their own chocolate bars. It's the perfect place to unwind, take in the scenery, and temporarily get away from the busy metropolis.

- **The Cologne Zoo** (Kölner Zoo) is a well-liked destination for families and animal lovers. It provides educational activities, animal exhibitions, interactive exhibits, and housing for a wide variety of animal species.

- **RheinEnergieStadion:** If you enjoy sports, you absolutely must go to the RheinEnergieStadion. The FC Cologne football team plays their home games there, and other events like concerts are also held there.

- **Rhine boat tours**: Seeing Cologne from the water is a very unique experience. Numerous businesses provide boat cruises along the Rhine River, enabling guests to take in the city's skyline, landmarks, and picturesque settings from a new angle.

- Hidden Gem. **El-De Haus / NS Documentation Center** is the site of the former headquarters of the Gestapo and is now a museum documenting those atrocities and the Third Reich in general in the region. It is an interesting stop for those wanting to learn more about this period.

Stuttgart

Stuttgart, the capital of the German state of Baden-Württemberg, is a vibrant city with a rich history and impressive tourist attractions. Here are some of the top highlights and must-visit places in Stuttgart:

- **The Mercedes-Benz Museum** is a recognizable museum that chronicles the fascinating history of one of the most well-known car companies in the world, Mercedes-Benz. It provides visitors with an engaging experience by housing a sizable collection of historic automobiles, exhibits, and interactive displays.

- **Porsche Museum**: This museum honors the illustrious sports car maker and is a must-see for auto aficionados. It has an amazing collection of Porsche vehicles, including classic models, futuristic vehicles, and racing legends.

- Art lovers can explore the remarkable collection of European paintings and sculptures from the 14th to the 21st century at the **Stuttgart State Gallery** (Staatsgalerie Stuttgart). Famous artists, including Monet, Picasso, Rembrandt, and many more, have pieces at the museum.

- **Stuttgart Palace (Schlossplatz)** is a magnificent Baroque building encircled by lovely grounds and is situated in the center of the city. It is an important historical site and the home of the Baden-Württemberg State Parliament.

- The **Wilhelma Zoo and Botanical Garden** is a rare example of a zoological and botanical garden combined. Visitors can take in the stunning sceneries and varied plant collections while admiring a wide range of animal species. The structure's Moorish-inspired architecture adds to the attraction's attractiveness.

- **Königstraße**: Stuttgart's primary shopping thoroughfare, this lively pedestrian street is home to a wide variety of stores, including boutiques, department stores, and coffee shops. It's a terrific location for leisurely strolls or a little retail therapy.

- The Stuttgart TV Tower (**Fernsehturm** Stuttgart) offers a bird's-eye perspective of the city and its environs. The observation deck, which is accessible by elevator, offers breathtaking views of the surrounding area from a height of more than 200 meters.

- **Weissenhof Estate** (Weißenhofsiedlung): The Weissenhof Estate is a UNESCO World Heritage site. It was created by notable architects, including Le Corbusier, Ludwig Mies van der Rohe, and Walter Gropius. It offers a look at the Bauhaus movement and displays modern architecture and urban design from the 1920s.

- **Solitude Palace (Schloss Solitude**) is a splendid rococo-style building encircled by enormous gardens. It overlooks Stuttgart from a hill. The palace complex is the perfect place for a tranquil day trip because it also has a hunting lodge, stables, and a lovely park.

- If you happen to be in Stuttgart in late September or early October, don't miss the Stuttgart Beer Festival (Cannstatter Volksfest). After Oktoberfest in Munich, it is the second-largest beer festival in Germany and features traditional beer tents, fairground rides, and delectable regional food.

- Hidden Gem. **The Old Castle, Altes Schloss**, is a historic fortress located in Stuttgart, near the center. Dating back to the Renaissance period, it is a wonderful reminder of the city's incredible history.

Dresden

Dresden, the capital city of the German state of Saxony, is known for its rich history, stunning architecture, and cultural heritage. Here are some of the top tourist attractions and highlights in Dresden:

- **Zwinger Palace**: One of Dresden's most recognizable features is this majestic palace. The Old Masters Picture Gallery and the Porcelain Collection are two of the several museums housed in this spectacular late 17th-century baroque structure.

- **Frauenkirche: The Church of Our Lady**, often known as the Frauenkirche, represents Dresden's resiliency and regeneration. It was completely rebuilt after being destroyed during World War II and reopened in 2005. Its stunning dome provides sweeping views of the city.

- **Semper Opera House**: Known for its stunning architecture and exceptional performances, the Semper Opera House is regarded as one of the most spectacular opera houses in the world. It features opera, ballet, and classical music performances all year long.

- **Dresden Castle**: This magnificent castle complex is home to a number of museums, including the Royal Palace Museum, highlighting the history and culture of Saxony, and the Green Vault, housing an extraordinary collection of treasures.

- **The Royal Palace Gardens** are a tranquil retreat from the busy city and are located next to the Dresden Castle. The gardens are exquisitely designed and make for the perfect location for a picnic or leisurely stroll.

- **Pillnitz Palace and Park**: Pillnitz Palace, a spectacular example of Chinese-inspired architecture, is situated on the outskirts of Dresden. Huge gardens, including the well-known Camellia Grove and the Palm House, surround the palace.

- **The Dresden Transport Museum** is a must-see for anybody interested in transportation. It contains a sizable collection of vintage autos, locomotives, trams, and other transportation.

- The center of Dresden's Old Town is the famous **Neumarkt Square**. It has remarkable architecture, including the Dresden City Museum, the reconstructed Frauenkirche, and numerous cafes and restaurants.

- **The Dresden Panometer**, designed by artist Yadegar Asisi, provides a singular panoramic perspective of the city throughout its history. Dresden's past is fascinatingly revealed via the 360-degree artwork.

- **Saxony-Elb Valley**: The Elbe Valley is a lovely region along the river that has been named a UNESCO World Heritage Site. It offers options for cycling, hiking, and boat cruises, as well as lovely scenery and attractive vineyards.

Frankfurt

Frankfurt, a vibrant city in Germany, offers a blend of historical charm and modern attractions. Frankfurt suffered a great deal of damage during World War II; however, it was reconstructed in the city square much in the way it had been prior. Here are some of the tourist highlights and attractions you can explore in Frankfurt:

- **Römerberg**: The center of Frankfurt's old town lies this famous square. There are charming half-timbered homes there, notably the well-known Römer, the city hall. There are markets, cafes, and restaurants in the bustling Römerberg neighborhood.

- **St. Bartholomew's Cathedral**, sometimes called the Frankfurt Cathedral, is a magnificent Gothic building that was built in the fourteenth century. Climbing the tower will provide visitors with sweeping views of the city.

- **Palmengarten**: This stunning 54-acre botanical park is home to a diverse range of international plant varieties. It is a fantastic location for relaxing, exploring themed gardens, and taking in seasonal flower displays.

- **Museumsufer**: The Museumsufer (Museum Embankment), which is a collection of museums presenting art, history, and culture, is situated on the banks of the River Main. The Städel Museum, the German Film Museum, and the Museum of Modern Art are a few significant institutions (MMK).

- **Goethe House and Museum**: Johann Wolfgang von Goethe, one of Germany's most well-known authors, was born here. Visitors can explore the rooms where Goethe spent his formative years and learn more about his life and works thanks to the house's preservation as a museum.

- **Main Tower**: At 200 meters tall, the Main Tower is the only skyscraper in Frankfurt that is accessible to the general public. Beautiful panoramic views of the town, including the business area and the River Main, may be seen from its observation deck.

- **Kleinmarkthalle**: This thriving indoor market is a must-visit location for foodies. A variety of fresh products, regional specialties, international cuisine, and homegrown food vendors selling mouthwatering snacks are available at Kleinmarkthalle.

- One of Germany's largest natural history museums is the **Senckenberg** Natural History Museum. Numerous fossils, minerals, and animal specimens are kept there, including the renowned T-Rex skeleton.

- If you're in the market for some retail therapy, head to Frankfurt's largest shopping district, **Zeil**. Department stores, boutiques, foreign fashion labels, and a variety of dining establishments are all located here.

- **Ebbelwei Express**: The Ebbelwei Express is a vintage tram that offers tours of Frankfurt while pouring the regional apple wine, also known as Ebbelwei. It is a unique experience.

- Hidden Gem. The **Kleinmarkthalle** is a vibrant indoor market with over 150 stalls. The local delicacies are incredible. Make sure you come when you are ready to eat.

- Hidden Gem. **Lohrberg Schanke** is Franfkurt's lone vineyard, just barely outside Frankfurt proper. It offers an incredible view of the Frankfurt skyline and insight into the Germany winemaking tradition.

Bremen

Bremen, located in northern Germany, is a city with a rich history, charming architecture, and a vibrant cultural scene. Here are some of the top tourist attractions and highlights in Bremen:

- The Roland Statue and Bremen Town Hall are both remarkable Gothic structures from the 15th century. Bremen Town Hall is a UNESCO World Heritage Site. The famous Roland Statue, which represents Bremen's trading freedom and liberties, is located nearby.

- One of the oldest buildings in northern Germany is **Bremen Cathedral (St. Peter's Cathedral)**, a majestic cathedral built in the Romanesque style. Visitors can explore the crypt, climb the tower for panoramic views, and admire the fantastic architecture.

- The **Schnoor** is Bremen's oldest neighborhood and is distinguished by its twisting, winding streets surrounded by charming half-timbered homes. This neighborhood is ideal for taking leisurely strolls, going boutique shopping, and visiting quaint cafés and eateries.

- **Böttcherstraße** is a distinctive architectural ensemble that includes expressionist buildings, museums, galleries, and stores. It is referred to as Bremen's "Street of Art and Culture." It is a thriving center of culture that must not be overlooked.

- **Universum Science Center**: The Universum offers interactive exhibitions on subjects including human biology, technology, and the environment. It is a well-liked destination for both kids and adults. It's an interactive learning experience that mixes knowledge and enjoyment.

- **Bremen Roland Music Hall** is a musical venue with a stellar reputation for incredible acoustics that frequently accommodates classical, jazz, and pop events. It's a fantastic location to take in the energetic local music scene.

- **Beck's Brewery**: Bremen has a rich brewing history, and a trip there might provide insight into how beer is made. Take a tour to discover the brewery's past, view the facilities used for production, and sample some beer.

- **The Weser River** flows through Bremen, and the city's riverbank features stunning views, lovely promenades, and bustling eateries and bars. Stroll along the embankment and take in the seaside ambiance of the city.

- **Botanika** is a unique botanical garden that displays several plant species from all over the world. It is situated in the

Rhododendron Park. It has interactive exhibitions, themed gardens, and a butterfly house.

- The ethnographic and natural history museum in Bremen, **Übersee-Museum Bremen**, takes visitors on a tour of the world while examining various cultures, species of animals, and ecosystems. It is an engaging experience thanks to its varied collections and interactive exhibits.

Freiburg

Hidden Gem Freiburg, located in southwestern Germany, is a picturesque city known for its historic charm, beautiful scenery, and vibrant culture. Considered by many to be "The" Black Forest City, it is somewhat of a Hidden Gem as it tends to be off most travelers' radar. Some of the top tourist attractions and highlights in Freiburg follow:

- **Freiburg Minster**: The city's recognizable cathedral and one of its most recognizable landmarks are the Freiburg Minster or Freiburger Münster. At the summit, its imposing spire provides sweeping views of the city and dominates the skyline.

- **Schlossberg**: The Schlossberg, a hill in the center of Freiburg, provides breathtaking views over the city and its surroundings. You can hike or take the Schlossbergbahn funicular to get to the top. The ruins of a historic castle are also located on the hill.

- The **Colombischlössle Archaeological Museum** presents Freiburg's and the surrounding area's rich past. It offers knowledge about the city's past and houses archaeological relics, including Roman artifacts.

- The **Augustiner Museum** is well known for its collection of Renaissance and medieval artwork. It is a must-see for art fans because it has ornamental arts, sculptures, and paintings from many eras.

- **Mundenhof Animal Park**: On the outskirts of Freiburg, Mundenhof is a sizable animal park that provides a rare chance to watch a range of animals in their natural habitats. It's the ideal location for families and environment enthusiasts.

- **Black Forest**: Freiburg is situated on the outskirts of the Black Forest, a sizable and alluring region renowned for its thick forests, quaint towns, and picturesque vistas. While visiting Freiburg, you must explore the Black Forest, where there are options for riding, hiking, and taking in the scenery.

- **Schauinsland**: Schauinsland is a mountain close to Freiburg that offers stunning panoramas of the region. Freiburg Botanical Garden: The Botanical Garden of Freiburg University is a tranquil oasis that displays a wide range of plant species from all over the world. Visitors can ascend to the summit by cable car and take in panoramic views, go hiking, or even attempt paragliding. It's a wonderful spot to unwind, wander, and take in the wonders of nature.

- Freiburg's bustling **farmer's market** offers a variety of fresh vegetables, regional specialties, and handcrafted goods and is located in the city's Old Town. It's a great location to experience the local culture and savor some delectable delights.

- Hidden Gem – **Freiburg Bachle** are tunnels flowing along many streets that once brought fresh water into Freiburg. It's not really hidden, but these city landmarks are really rather cool and worth noticing.

Augsburg

Augsburg, located in Bavaria, Germany, is a historic city that offers a wealth of tourist attractions and highlights. It is a very short train ride from Munich, and many tie it in with their trip there, possibly on a day trip. A few things to see and do in Augsburg:

- **The Augsburg Town Hall**, also known as the Rathaus, is a magnificent Renaissance structure and one of the city's most recognizable buildings. It has a spectacular Golden Hall with ornate gold leaf embellishments and frescoes.

- **The Cathedral of St. Maria and St. Cyprian**, also called the Augsburg Cathedral (Dom), is a magnificent church in the Gothic style with a long history. Visitors can tour the stunning interior and ascend the tower for sweeping views of Augsburg, and its twin towers which dominate the city skyline.

- **Fuggerei**: The oldest social settlement in the world, Fuggerei is a distinctive communal housing development. Established by the Fugger family in the sixteenth century, it is made up of vibrant homes arranged in a grid. Wandering the streets allows visitors to see a glimpse into the daily life of the locals.

- The **Augsburger Puppenkiste** is a well-known puppet theater that has mesmerized audiences for many years. It features a range of puppet presentations, including conventional fairy tales and timeless tales, making both kids and adults happy.

- **Schaezlerpalais**: The German Baroque Gallery is located in the magnificent Schaezlerpalais (Deutsche Barockgalerie). It exhibits an amazing selection of Baroque-era works of art, including works by well-known creators such as Rembrandt, Rubens, and Goya.

- **Perlachturm**: A tower from the Middle Ages, the Perlachturm provides stunning views over Augsburg. The tower's stairs allow visitors to ascend and take in panoramic views over the city's historic district, including its landmarks, churches, and rooftops.

- **Botanischer** Garten Augsburg: This stunning botanical park features a wide variety of plant species from all over the world. Visitors can explore numerous themed gardens, including a Japanese garden and a Mediterranean garden, and it offers a tranquil setting for leisurely strolls.

- **Maximilianmuseum**: The Maximilianmuseum is a museum of art and cultural history that highlights the rich history of Augsburg. It showcases the city's significance as a center of art and craftsmanship with a broad collection of sculptures, paintings, and antiquities.

- **Zoo Augsburg**: The family-friendly attraction Zoo Augsburg is home to a wide range of animals from several continents. While roaming through the zoo's expansive grounds, visitors can see animals including lions, elephants, penguins, and many others.

- **Lech River**: The Lech River, which runs through Augsburg, provides beautiful scenery and leisure options. The city's charms can be enjoyed from the water by taking a boat tour, taking a leisurely stroll along the riverbanks, or renting a bike to explore the gorgeous routes.

Bonn

Bonn, located in western Germany, is a charming city that offers a rich historical and cultural heritage. Here are some of the top tourist attractions and highlights in Bonn:

- Ludwig van Beethoven was born in Bonn, which is where he now called home for many years. A museum honoring Beethoven's life and work, the **Beethoven House (Beethoven-Haus)** displays his personal items, original manuscripts, and musical instruments.

- The beautiful Romanesque church known as the **Bonn Minster (Bonner Münster)** is situated in the heart of the city. With its beautiful architecture and opulent interior, it is one of Bonn's most recognizable buildings. Ascending the church tower offers views of the entire city.

- **Poppelsdorf Building and Botanical Gardens**: Poppelsdorf Palace, also known as Poppelsdorfer Schloss, is a stunning palace from the 18th century that is surrounded by verdant botanical gardens. The gardens provide a tranquil haven for lovers of nature and are home to a wide variety of plant types.

- Rhine River banks are home to the sizable leisure area known as **Rheinaue Park**. It has large green spaces, beautiful lakes, and a range of recreational activities like biking, boating, and picnicking. Don't overlook the park's lovely Japanese Garden.

- **Bonn's Museum Mile (Museumsmeile)** is a center of culture that is home to quite a number of top-notch institutions. Highlights include the Kunst- und Ausstellungshalle der Bundesrepublik Deutschland (Kunst- und Ausstellungshalle der Bundesrepublik Deutschland), the Haus der Geschichte (Museum of Contemporary History), and the Bundeskunsthalle (which exhibits a variety of art exhibitions).

- **Bonn Old Town**: Wander around Bonn's lovely Old Town (Altstadt), highlighted by small shops, winding lanes, and old structures. Visit the Marktplatz, the city's main square, where you can discover the Beethoven Monument and the Old Town Hall (Altes Rathaus).

- **Drachenburg Castle (Schloss Drachenburg**) is a must-see sight just outside of Bonn, despite being outside of Bonn proper. The castle, which resembles something out of a fairytale, is perched on a hilltop overlooking the Rhine River and provides stunning views of the surroundings.

- **Cruises on the Rhine River**: The Rhine River runs through Bonn, and you may take a beautiful boat ride along it. Enjoy the beautiful scenery, little towns, and wineries that line the riverbanks. You can even learn about the history and sights of the area on some cruises that even include live commentary.

- Hidden Gem—Burg Drachenfels is a ruined 12th-century castle on top of a hill just outside Bonn. The castle and the hill have a lengthy history, with a heavy focus on dragon lore stories for which have been handed down for centuries.

Rostock

Rostock is a beautiful city located in northern Germany, known for its rich history, stunning architecture, and vibrant atmosphere. Here are some of the top tourist attractions and highlights in Rostock:

- **Rostock Old Town**: With its lovely cobblestone alleys, vibrant gabled homes, and medieval architecture, Rostock's historic center is a must-see. Discover the lively Neuer Markt (New Market) plaza and its surrounding spectacular structures, including the Town Hall and the St. Mary's Church.

- **Warnemünde**: A well-known beach resort and a component of Rostock, Warnemünde is situated on the Baltic Sea coast. Explore the quaint fishing village with its charming houses, stores, and restaurants, as well as the sandy beach and lighthouse for panoramic views.

- One of the oldest educational institutions in the world is **Rostock University**, which was established in 1419. Visit the main building, which has great architecture and a gorgeous courtyard, and take a stroll around its lovely campus.

- **Rostock Zoo** is one of the most well-liked attractions in the city and is located in the Barnstorfer Wald. Elephants, lions, giraffes, and penguins are among the many different species that call it home. The zoo also offers several educational programs and a petting zoo.

- **St. Peter's Church (Petrikirche**) is a magnificent work of architecture and is regarded as the highest brick Gothic church in the world. Climb the tower to get a bird' s-eye perspective of Rostock and the surroundings.

- The Rostock Schiffbau- und **Schifffahrtsmuseum** provides a fascinating look into the city's nautical past. Explore the displays of ship models, navigational tools, and relics associated with seafaring and shipbuilding.

- **Kröpeliner Tor**: The Kröpeliner Tor, dating to the 13th century, is one of the city's original gates. It is a well maintained medieval stronghold that represents Rostock's lengthy history.

- **City Harbor**: City Harbor in Rostock is a bustling waterfront neighborhood with a contemporary marina, eateries, bars, and stores. Enjoy a dinner while looking out over the harbor, rent a boat, or take a leisurely stroll along the promenade.

- **IGA Park**: IGA Park is a sizable recreation area with lovely gardens, walking paths, and an observation tower providing panoramic views on the outskirts of Rostock. It's the ideal location for a picnic or a peaceful day in the outdoors.

- Don't miss the **Hanse Sail festival** if you happen to be in Rostock in August. Tall ships, sailing boats, and traditional boats from all over the world participate in this annual event, which results in an amazing maritime display.

Potsdam

Potsdam, located just outside Berlin, Germany, is a city renowned for its rich history, stunning architecture, and beautiful landscapes. The city is known for its magnificent palaces, lush gardens, and UNESCO World Heritage Sites. Here are some of the top tourist attractions and highlights in Potsdam:

- The crown jewel of Potsdam and a must-see destination is the **Sanssouci Palace**. Sanssouci Palace is a magnificent example of rococo architecture and was constructed as a getaway for Frederick the Great, the king of Prussia. A gorgeous scene is created by its lovely terraced gardens, vineyards, and eccentric sculptures.

- **Sanssouci Park** is a large, beautiful parkland that covers more than 700 acres and is located next to the palace. It has elegant pavilions, elaborate fountains, and wonderfully designed gardens. A leisurely stroll through the park offers serene surroundings and breathtaking views.

- **The New Mansion (Neues Palais**), a magnificent Baroque palace located in Sanssouci Park, was built as a representation of Prussian might. The Marble Hall and the Grotto Hall, among other lavish interiors, are evidence of the riches and excess of the Prussian emperors.

- **Cecilienhof Palace**: The historical Potsdam Conference, which brought together international leaders, including Stalin, Truman, and Churchill, to address the post-World War II world, was held at this palace in 1945, making it significant historically. The palace is a remarkable attraction due to its charming setting on the Heiliger See coastlines and English Tudor-style architecture.

- **Babelsberg Palace and Park**: A charming palace with a fusion of Gothic, Renaissance, and Romantic architectural styles, Babelsberg Palace is located on the banks of the Havel River. Babelsberg Park, which is nearby, offers beautiful views of the river and a tranquil location for a leisurely stroll or picnic.

- **Dutch Quarter**: With more than 150 red-brick homes constructed in the Dutch architectural style, Potsdam's Dutch

Quarter is a distinctive neighborhood. Visitors can explore lovely stores, boutiques, cafes, and galleries by strolling through its winding alleyways.

- **Potsdam's Old Town**: Potsdam's Old Town's historic core is a fascinating region to explore. It has a charming ambience thanks to its cobblestone streets, vibrant homes, and welcoming squares. The Old Town Hall and the Church of St. Nicholas are prominent features of the Old Market Square (Alter Markt), which is remarkable.

- **Peacock Island**, a picturesque island in the Havel River, is a natural wonderland and a UNESCO World Heritage Site. The island's peaceful beauty may be appreciated by visitors, who can also stroll around its well landscaped gardens and see roaming peacocks.

- Hidden Gem – **Alexandrowka** is a quaint little Russian village built in the middle of Potsdam. Built in 1826, this enclave includes 14 farms and an Orthodox Church. An extremely unusual find in the heart of Potsdam.

Trier

Trier, for many, really is a **Hidden Gem** type of city. Located in western Germany, it is a city steeped in history and known as the "Rome of the North". It is one of the oldest cities in Germany and boasts an impressive array of well-preserved Roman ruins and other architectural gems, as follows below:

- The greatest Roman city gate north of the Alps and a UNESCO World Heritage site is **Porta Nigra**, a renowned city gate. It is a must-see sight due to its amazing size and architectural intricacies.

- The magnificent **Trier Cathedral (Dom St. Peter)**, built in the fourth century, is renowned for its fusion of Romanesque,

Gothic, and Baroque architectural styles. This is where the Holy Robe, which is thought to be Jesus's tunic, is preserved.

- **Amphitheater**: Investigate the remnants of this 20,000-seat amphitheater from the time of the Roman Empire. Today, it serves as a location for a variety of concerts and cultural activities and remains an excellent location to visit and walk through and around.

- Visit the remnants of the **Roman Imperial Baths (Kaiserthermen)**, which were once the biggest in the Roman Empire. The striking ruins shed light on the opulent bathing tradition of ancient times.

- **Basilica of Constantine**: Originally a throne room, this Roman basilica is now a museum. Its enormous size and splendor attest to Trier's prominence during the Roman era.

- Discover the Baroque beauty of the **Electoral Palace (Kurfürstliches Palais)**, the former home of the prince-electors of Trier. The Rheinisches Landesmuseum, which highlights Trier's rich history, is now housed in the palace.

- Visit **Karl Marx's birthplace** to learn more about this significant philosopher, economist, and social theorist. The museum offers details about his life and creative output.

- **St. Gangolf's Church**: Take in the impressive tower and exquisite interior of this example of medieval architecture. From its tower, the church provides sweeping views of the city.

- Explore the vibrant **Hauptmarkt**, Trier's main square, which is flanked by colorful buildings and lined with cafes and shops. This is a wonderful location to take in the ambiance and sample the local fare.

- Visit the **Rheinische Landesmuseum** to fully immerse yourself in Trier's past. It contains a sizable collection of historical exhibits, artwork, and archaeological objects from the Roman, medieval, and modern eras of the city.

Baden-Baden

Baden-Baden is a charming town located in southwestern Germany, known for its natural beauty, historic architecture, and luxurious spas. some of the top tourist attractions and highlights in Baden-Baden are:

- **Kurhaus**: A cultural and social hub in Baden, the Kurhaus is a stunning structure. It has beautiful architecture, notably the renowned Kurhaus colonnade, a large casino, and elegant gardens. Throughout the year, the Kurhaus organizes a number of occasions, performances, and exhibitions.

- For those who enjoy the outdoors, you must visit **Lichtentaler Allee**. The Lichtentaler Allee is a charming boulevard that runs alongside the Oos River and is decorated with lovely flowers, tree-lined walkways, and tasteful sculptures. It's the perfect location for a picnic or leisurely stroll.

- The **Caracalla Spa** is one of the most well-liked spas in the city. Baden-Baden is well-known for its thermal baths. The spa provides a selection of tranquil pools, saunas, steam rooms, and wellness services. It's the ideal location for relaxation and rejuvenation.

- Visit Friedrichsbad for a distinctive bathing experience. This ancient Roman-Irish bathhouse has been in use since 1877 and adheres to customary bathing practices. Visitors can enjoy thermal baths, showers, and massages in a gorgeously restored environment.

- If you're feeling lucky, visit the **Baden-Baden Casino**, one of the most prominent and historic casinos in all of Europe. Visitors can test their luck at numerous games of chance at the casino, which is housed inside the Kurhaus and offers an opulent and glamorous ambiance.

- Visit the summit of **Merkur Mountain** for amazing views of Baden-Baden and the surrounding countryside. The peak is accessible by hiking or a less strenuous funicular railway. Once you get to the top, you'll be richly rewarded with magnificent views and a welcoming mountain restaurant.

- **Museum Frieder Burda**: Home to a noteworthy collection of modern and contemporary art, the Museum Frieder Burda is a must-visit destination for art fans. The museum features pieces by well-known painters such Jackson Pollock, Pablo Picasso, and Gerhard Richter.

- **Staatliche Kunsthalle**: The Staatliche Kunsthalle is a contemporary art gallery that regularly hosts exhibitions by well-known and up-and-coming artists, making it another art location well worth visiting. The gallery emphasizes a variety of artistic mediums, such as painting, sculpture, photography, and video art.

Nuremberg

Germany's Bavaria state is home to the historic and culturally significant city of Nuremberg. Nuremberg attracts tourists from all over the world with a variety of tourist attractions that are known for their medieval architecture, lively markets, and important historical monuments, the main highlights of which are listed below:

- **Nuremberg Castle (Kaiserburg)** is a spectacular stronghold from the Middle Ages that is perched on a hill overlooking the city. Visitors can take in the spectacular views of Nuremberg while exploring the complex's different buildings, towers, and courtyards.

- The attractive **Old Town of Nuremberg (Altstadt)** is a beautifully preserved medieval neighborhood with winding cobblestone lanes, half-timbered homes, and picturesque squares. Visitors can explore the colorful street markets, see the well-known **Frauenkirche** (Church of Our Lady), and take in the stunning architecture while strolling around this neighborhood.

- The **Nuremberg Christmas Market (Christkindlesmarkt)**, which takes place every year, is one of the most well-known in Germany and attracts tourists from all over the world. The market's numerous stands selling traditional crafts, presents, and delectable foods like gingerbread and mulled wine create a magical holiday ambiance.

- **Documentation Center Reichsparteitagsgelände**: This museum provides information about the city's somber past during the Nazi era. The exhibition, which is housed in the former Congress Hall, offers a comprehensive look at the rise and fall of the Nazi government, making it a significant educational location.

- The **St. Lorenz Church** is one of Nuremberg's most well-known attractions. It is an amazing Gothic structure. Because of its complex stone carvings and breathtaking stained glass windows, it is a must-see for anyone who enjoys art and architecture.

- **Albrecht Dürer's House**: The renowned German Renaissance artist Albrecht Dürer's former home has been turned into a museum. Visitors can go around Dürer's residence and workspace, see his works of art, and discover more about his enormous contributions to the field of art.

- The **Spielzeugmuseum** in Nuremberg is a toy museum that houses a sizable collection of toys from various historical periods. It is a treat for both kids and adults and provides an intriguing voyage through the history of toys.

- **Zoo in Nuremberg (Nürnberger Tiergarten)**: The Nuremberg Zoo is spread out over a vast area and is home to around 3,000 species from all over the world. It features a wide variety of exhibits, including large cats, primates, birds, and marine life, giving visitors of all ages an enjoyable and instructive experience.

- Hidden Gem – **Hangman's Bridge (Henkersteg)** is a wonderful and authentic wooden bridge that was once the home of the city's hangman. Nice historical overview of the city from the era as well

Düsseldorf

Germany's Düsseldorf, a thriving city with a rich cultural past and bustling shopping streets, is situated on the banks of the Rhine. Another city that was destroyed during World War II but rebuilt, some sites are as follows:

- The **Rheinturm** is a renowned communications tower that provides stunning 360-degree views over Düsseldorf. The observation deck, which is 170 meters above the ground and accessible by elevator, offers visitors breathtaking views of the town and the River Rhine.

- **Königsallee** (Kö): Königsallee, sometimes known as the "Kö," is a well-known shopping street in Berlin. This attractive strip is adorned with high-end fashion businesses, luxury labels, and superb jewelry stores. The Kö is particularly well-known for its charming canal that runs down its middle and is lined with lovely bridges and trees.

- **MedienHafen** (Media Harbor): The MedienHafen is a cutting-edge neighborhood that highlights Düsseldorf's talent for building and design. The region is home to cutting-edge structures created by well-known architects like Frank Gehry. Visitors can stroll along the harbor's promenade, take in the distinctive architecture, and savor a choice of eateries, coffee shops, and pubs.

- **Schloss Benrath (Benrath Palace)** is a magnificent baroque palace encircled by lovely grounds, located in the southern portion of Düsseldorf. Visitors can stroll through the expansive grounds, which include a French garden and an English landscape garden, and take guided tours of the palace's sumptuous interiors.

- **North Rhine-Westphalia Art Collection**, also known as the **Kunstsammlung** Nordrhein-Westfalen, is a prominent art museum with three locations: K20, K21, and the Schmela Haus. Art lovers shouldn't miss it. The collection features a wide variety of modern and contemporary art, including pieces by well-known creators like Pablo Picasso, Andy Warhol, and Joseph Beuys.

- **Aquazoo-Löbbecke Museum**: This remarkable fusion of a zoo and a natural history museum is known as the Aquazoo-Löbbecke Museum. Fish, reptiles, mammals, birds, and other aquatic and land species are all housed there. The museum also has exhibits that teach visitors about the evolution of the planet's ecosystems.

- Hidden Gem – **Rheinwerft** and drinks along the Rhine River. Make your way down to the banks of the Rhine and find a place that most appeals to what you are looking for, have a seat, and watch the sunset across the Rhine.

Hanover

Visitors can discover a range of tourist sites and landmarks in Hanover, the capital city of Lower Saxony in Germany. Not as frequented as many other locations there are some attractions as follows:

- Hanover visitors should not miss the exquisite baroque **Herrenhausen Gardens**. The gardens have beautiful fountains, statues, and flowerbeds with vibrant colors. The two main attractions are the Great Garden, with its well-known cascades, and the **Berggarten**, which has a botanical garden and the Herrenhausen Palace.

- **Hanover Zoo**: One of Germany's oldest and largest zoos, Hanover Zoo is a well-liked destination for tourists of all ages. Over 3,000 animals of different sorts, including elephants, giraffes, lions, penguins, and many more, may be seen in the zoo. Additionally, it provides educational activities and interactive exhibitions.

- **Old Town Hanover**: The Old Town of Hanover is a lovely neighborhood with winding lanes, old structures, and picturesque squares. You can tour the Old Town Hall and the Market Church of St. George, two renowned landmarks, here. There are a ton of cafes, restaurants, and stores throughout the Old Town.

- **Maschsee**: Hanover's city center is home to the sizable man-made lake known as Maschsee. It is a well-liked location for outdoor pursuits like jogging, cycling, boating, and strolling. Additionally, you can unwind along the lakeside promenade, have a picnic, or go to a lakeside cafe.

- **Hanover State Opera**: The Hanover State Opera is a must-visit for anybody interested in cultural activities. Opera, ballet, and classical concerts are just a few of the performances that are presented in the opera house. Even if you don't go to a performance, the building is worth seeing because it is a work of art in architecture.

- **Sprengel Museum**: The Sprengel Museum, which has a sizable collection of modern and contemporary art, is a must-see for art fans. The museum displays the creations of well-known painters like Picasso, Klee, Kandinsky, and Nolde. Additionally, it offers educational activities and changing exhibitions.

- **Hanover Adventure Zoo**: This unusual zoo blends adventure aspects with conventional animal exhibitions. Themed sections like Gorilla Mountain, Jungle Palace, and Zambezi boat trip are available for visitors to enjoy. The zoo provides a variety of participatory activities, entertaining shows, and wildlife encounters.

- **Sea Life Hanover** is an aquarium in the heart of the city that lets tourists explore the wonderful underwater world. It has a variety of aquatic ecosystems, including a walkthrough tunnel where you can get up close and personal with sharks, turtles, and vibrant fish.

- **Hanover New Town Hall**: The New Town Hall is a striking structure that dominates Hanover's skyline. It has magnificent architecture and provides sweeping views of the city from its dome.

- Hidden Gem – The **Aegidien Church War Memorial** is a burned-out frame of a church that was incinerated during World War II but stands as a monument to those whose lives were lost during the war.

Leipzig

Leipzig, located in eastern Germany, is a vibrant city known for its rich history, cultural heritage, and thriving arts scene. Here are some of the top tourist attractions and highlights in Leipzig:

- **St. Thomas Church (Thomaskirche)** is a well-known church that is well-known for its association with Johann Sebastian Bach, who oversaw the music for more than 25 years. Visitors can check out the stunning church interior and attend concerts by Bach's St. Thomas Boys Choir.

- One of the oldest and most well-known zoos in the world, **Leipzig Zoo (Zoologischer Garten Leipzig)** is home to a vast diversity of species from all seven continents. It features a variety of displays, including the well-known Gondwanaland, a model of a tropical rainforest.

- The Battle of Leipzig in 1813, a crucial incident in the Napoleonic Wars, is commemorated by the monumental monument known as the **Battle of the Nations Memorial (Völkerschlachtdenkmal)**. Visitors can ascend to the top for sweeping views of the city and to learn more about the battle's historical setting.

- **Leipzig Botanical Garden (Leipziger Botanischer Garten)**: This 4.5-hectare botanical garden is a tranquil oasis with a wide variety of plants and flowers. It has a pond, greenhouses, and many themed gardens.

- Explore the quaint streets of **Leipzig's Old Town (Leipziger Altstadt)**, which are lined with beautifully renovated structures, cafes, and shops. The Renaissance-style Old Town Hall, the medieval Market Square, and the renowned Auerbachs Keller, a historic inn, are a few notable highlights.

- Art lovers shouldn't miss the **Museum of Fine Arts (Museum der Bildenden Künste)**, which has a remarkable collection of European artwork stretching from the Middle Ages to modern pieces. It features pieces by well-known artists like Monet, Rubens, and Rembrandt.

- The **Panometer** in Leipzig is a distinctive attraction that hosts sizable panoramic art exhibitions. Yadegar Asisi's stunning 360-degree installations feature historical imagery, such as the Amazon Rainforest or Leipzig in 1813.

- Opera and music enthusiasts will appreciate a trip to **Leipzig's Opera House**, which offers world-class performances and displays the abilities of the Leipzig Opera Ballet. The location is a work of art in architecture.

- Band from the Leipzig Gewandhaus: **The Leipzig Gewandhaus** Orchestra performs at the Gewandhaus music venue and is regarded as one of the best orchestras in the world. For music lovers, going to a classical music performance here is a must.

- **Stadtgeschichtliches Museum Leipzig (Limburg Museum of City History)**: This museum provides an engaging tour through Leipzig's past by presenting relics, interactive exhibits, and multimedia presentations that emphasize the city's evolution over time.

I have a couple of more cities that I really do consider hidden gems, and they often go unnoticed by many visitors despite their appeal. **Heidelberg** is one of these cities and is located a very short distance from Frankfurt. As it escaped World War II virtually unscathed, it still maintains its charm and historical sites, including the Old Town (Alstadt) and the marvelous castle of Schloss Heidelberg…and really, much more.

Aachen is the city, a short 35-minute train ride from Cologne (Koln). As the first city in Germany that was taken by the Allies during WWII, it was extensively damaged, but the old city charm and buildings are all in standing in their former glory, including the impressive City Hall (Rathaus), the massive Aachen Cathedral, and more. For those interested in World War II history, the remains of the West Wall can be seen just outside of town, the Dragon's Teeth in particular. Also, a short drive away (15 min or so) is the 3 corners area where Germany, Netherlands, and Belgium all come together, also a very nice and unique stop.

Chapter 3: Itineraries

As with any set itinerary provided by a third party, it is very hard to know what the travelers want to see. Is the traveler interested in seeing as many cities and towns as possible, or does the traveler wish to explore two cities deeply (if the latter is the case, we would recommend Munich and Berlin)?

Here's a sample five-day itinerary for Germany, covering some popular destinations. Really, these are our 5 chosen cities with destinations therein to see. Appreciation needs to be given to the fact that travel time has not been considered, and as teleportation is yet to be a thing, a 5-day itinerary may actually be 7, and a 7-day closer to 10.

Day 1: Berlin

- Start your trip in Berlin, the capital city of Germany.

- Visit iconic landmarks such as Brandenburg Gate, Berlin Wall, and Checkpoint Charlie.

- Explore Museum Island, home to several world-class museums like Pergamon Museum and Neues Museum.

- Take a stroll along Unter den Linden boulevard and visit the impressive Berlin Cathedral.

- In the evening, experience Berlin's vibrant nightlife in areas like Kreuzberg or Prenzlauer Berg.

Day 2: Munich

- Fly or take a train to Munich, known for its rich history and Bavarian charm.

- Explore the historic center, Marienplatz, and witness the famous Glockenspiel show at the New Town Hall.

- Visit the renowned Nymphenburg Palace and its beautiful gardens.

- Enjoy a traditional Bavarian meal and sample local beer at one of Munich's beer gardens.

- If time permits, consider visiting the Dachau Concentration Camp Memorial Site located just outside the city.

Day 3: Cologne

- Travel to Cologne, famous for its magnificent Cologne Cathedral.

- Explore the Gothic-style Cologne Cathedral and climb to the top for stunning city views.

- Take a walk along the Rhine River promenade and visit the historic Old Town (Altstadt).

- Don't miss the opportunity to sample Kölsch, the local beer brewed in Cologne.

- Consider visiting the Chocolate Museum (Schokoladenmuseum) to satisfy your sweet tooth.

Day 4: Hamburg

- Fly or take a train to Hamburg, a vibrant city with a rich maritime history.

- Visit the iconic Miniatur Wunderland, the world's largest model railway exhibition.

- Explore the historic warehouse district (Speicherstadt) and take a boat tour through the canals.

- Visit the Elbphilharmonie, an impressive concert hall with panoramic views of the city.

- Enjoy the nightlife and entertainment options in the lively St. Pauli district.

Day 5: Heidelberg

- Travel to Heidelberg, a picturesque city known for its historic university and castle.

- Explore the charming Old Town (Altstadt) with its narrow streets and baroque architecture.

- Visit Heidelberg Castle and enjoy panoramic views of the city and the Neckar River.

- Take a leisurely walk along the Philosopher's Walk for scenic views of the city and the castle.

- Before departing, indulge in some local delicacies at one of the traditional restaurants.

One week itinerary

Day 1: Berlin

- Start your trip in Germany's capital city, Berlin.

- Visit iconic landmarks such as the Brandenburg Gate, Reichstag Building, and Checkpoint Charlie.

- Explore Museum Island, home to several world-class museums.

- Take a stroll along the East Side Gallery, a section of the Berlin Wall adorned with colorful murals.

Day 2: Hamburg

- Travel to Hamburg, known for its vibrant harbor and maritime history.

- Visit the historic Speicherstadt, a UNESCO World Heritage site.

- Explore the HafenCity district and take a boat tour of the harbor.

- Enjoy the lively atmosphere of the St. Pauli neighborhood and the famous Reeperbahn.

Day 3: Cologne

- Journey to Cologne and visit its most famous landmark, the Cologne Cathedral (Kölner Dom).

- Take a walk along the Rhine River promenade and enjoy the view.

- Explore the charming Old Town (Altstadt) with its narrow streets and traditional buildings.

- Visit the Chocolate Museum (Schokoladenmuseum) and learn about the history of chocolate.

Day 4: Munich

- Fly or take a train to Munich, Bavaria's capital city.

- Explore the historic city center, including Marienplatz with its famous Glockenspiel.

- Visit the beautiful Nymphenburg Palace and its surrounding gardens.

- Discover Munich's beer culture by visiting a traditional beer garden or the Hofbräuhaus.

Day 5: Neuschwanstein Castle and the Bavarian Alps

- Take a day trip to the fairy-tale Neuschwanstein Castle, located in the picturesque Bavarian Alps.

- Enjoy the stunning views of the castle from the Marienbrücke (Mary's Bridge).

- Take a leisurely walk or hike in the surrounding area to appreciate the natural beauty.

Day 6: Heidelberg and the Rhine Valley

- Travel to Heidelberg and explore its well-preserved Old Town.

- Visit Heidelberg Castle and enjoy panoramic views of the city and the Neckar River.

- In the afternoon, take a scenic drive along the Rhine Valley and visit charming towns like Rüdesheim and Bacharach.

Day 7: Dresden

- Conclude your trip with a visit to Dresden, known as the "Florence on the Elbe."

- Explore the historic center and admire the impressive architecture of landmarks like the Frauenkirche and the Zwinger Palace.

- Visit the Green Vault (Grünes Gewölbe) to see its stunning collection of treasures.

- Take a stroll along the banks of the Elbe River and enjoy the city's vibrant atmosphere.

Chapter 4: Best Restaurants and Cuisine

Germany is renowned for having a wide range of gastronomic traditions. The following list of Germany's top 10 regional dishes includes some ideas for where to find them:

1. Bratwurst: A popular German sausage, often grilled or pan-fried. You can find bratwurst at street food stalls, beer gardens, and traditional German restaurants throughout the country.

2. Sauerkraut: Fermented cabbage served as a side dish to various meat dishes. Look for sauerkraut in traditional German restaurants, particularly those specializing in hearty German cuisine.

3. Pretzels: A type of baked bread product, usually twisted into a knot shape. Pretzels can be found in bakeries, street food stalls, and beer gardens across Germany.

4. Sauerbraten: A pot roast typically made from beef, marinated in a mixture of vinegar, water, and spices. You can try sauerbraten at traditional German restaurants, especially in the regions of Rhineland and Franconia.

5. Kartoffelsuppe (Potato Soup): This comforting soup is made with potatoes and vegetables and often accompanied by sausage or bacon. You can find delicious potato soup in local German pubs, known as "Gasthäuser," or traditional German restaurants.

6. Maultaschen: Swabian-style dumplings filled with meat, spinach, and spices. Look for maultaschen in restaurants in the Swabian region, particularly in cities like Stuttgart and Tübingen.

7. Königsberger Klopse: Meatballs made with ground veal or pork, served in a creamy caper sauce. You can try this specialty in traditional restaurants in the city of Königsberg (now Kaliningrad, Russia) or German restaurants that feature regional cuisines.

8. Schwarzwälder Kirschtorte (Black Forest Cake): A famous German dessert made with layers of chocolate cake, whipped cream, and cherries soaked in Kirsch (cherry brandy). You can find Black Forest Cake in pastry shops, cafés, and bakeries across Germany.

9. Flammkuchen: A thin, crispy pizza-like dish topped with crème fraîche, onions, and bacon. Look for Flammkuchen in restaurants specializing in Alsatian or southwestern German cuisine, such as in the regions of Baden-Württemberg and Alsace.

10. Spätzle: Soft egg noodles are commonly served as a side dish or main course. You can find spätzle in traditional German restaurants, particularly in the southern regions of Germany like Baden-Württemberg and Bavaria.

Restaurants

- Restaurant Tim Raue (Berlin): Located in Berlin, Restaurant Tim Raue is renowned for its Asian-inspired cuisine. Chef Tim Raue combines traditional Asian flavors with modern techniques, creating dishes like "Ma-Po-Tofu" (a spicy tofu dish) and "Kung Pao Chicken" (a stir-fried chicken dish with peanuts and chili).

- Schwarzwaldstube (Baiersbronn): Situated in Baiersbronn, Schwarzwaldstube is a Michelin three-star restaurant known for its gourmet German cuisine. The menu features exquisite dishes like "Roasted Venison with Red Cabbage and Dumplings" and "Lobster with Quail Egg and Champagne Sauce."

- Restaurant Bareiss (Baiersbronn): Also located in Baiersbronn, Restaurant Bareiss is another Michelin three-star establishment. The restaurant offers creative German cuisine, and guests can savor dishes such as "Loin of Milk-Fed Veal with Sweetbread" and "Gâteau of Goose Liver with Truffle."

- Aqua (Wolfsburg): Aqua, situated in Wolfsburg, is a Michelin three-star restaurant led by chef Sven Elverfeld. The restaurant showcases innovative and artfully presented dishes such as "Foie Gras with Cherries and Almonds" and "Suckling Pig with Parsley Root."

- Vendôme (Bergisch Gladbach): Located in Bergisch Gladbach, Vendôme is a Michelin three-star restaurant helmed by chef Joachim Wissler. The restaurant offers imaginative modern German cuisine, featuring dishes like "Roasted Scallops with Cauliflower and Yuzu" and "Lamb with Artichokes and Almonds."

- Tantris (Munich): Situated in Munich, Tantris is a renowned Michelin three-star restaurant known for its avant-garde French and international cuisine. Guests can enjoy dishes like "Lobster with Beetroot and Horseradish" and "Roasted Saddle of Venison with Pumpkin and Pomegranate."

- Restaurant Überfahrt Christian Jürgens (Rottach-Egern): Found in Rottach-Egern, Restaurant Überfahrt Christian Jürgens is a

Michelin three-star restaurant known for modern interpretations of Bavarian cuisine. Dishes include "Fillet of Char with Caraway and Spinach" and "Veal with Cucumber and Morels."

- Restaurant Amador (Mannheim): Located in Mannheim, Restaurant Amador is a Michelin three-star restaurant led by chef Juan Amador. It offers innovative and molecular cuisine, featuring dishes like "Marinated Mackerel with Tomato Water and Basil" and "Iberian Pork with Coconut and Mango."

- Waldhotel Sonnora (Wittlich): Located in Wittlich, Waldhotel Sonnora is a Michelin three-star restaurant renowned for its innovative German cuisine. Guests can enjoy dishes that incorporate seasonal ingredients and showcase culinary creativity.

Chapter 5: Accommodations in Germany

Germany offers various accommodation options to suit different budgets, preferences, and travel styles. Here are some common types of accommodation you can find in Germany:

- Hotels: Germany has a vast selection of hotels ranging from budget-friendly options to luxury establishments. Major cities like Berlin, Munich, and Frankfurt have a wide range of international hotel chains, boutique hotels, and family-run accommodations. Hotels in Germany typically offer amenities such as private bathrooms, breakfast options, and sometimes on-site restaurants or bars.

- Guesthouses/Pensions: Guesthouses or pensions are smaller, family-run accommodations that provide a more intimate and personalized experience. They are often located in rural areas or smaller towns and can offer a homely atmosphere with comfortable rooms and traditional German hospitality.

- Bed and Breakfast (B&B): B&Bs are popular in Germany, especially in rural regions and scenic areas. They usually offer cozy rooms with breakfast included in the price. B&Bs can be found in charming countryside locations or even within historic buildings.

- Holiday Apartments/Vacation Rentals: Renting a holiday apartment or vacation rental can be an excellent option, especially for families or those seeking more space and the convenience of a kitchen. Websites like Airbnb, HomeAway, and Booking.com offer a variety of apartments and vacation homes throughout Germany.

- Hostels: Germany has a well-established hostel culture, making it a popular choice for budget travelers and backpackers. Hostels provide shared dormitory-style rooms or private rooms with shared facilities. They often have communal areas, kitchens, and social activities, making them an excellent option for meeting fellow travelers.

- Camping: If you prefer the outdoors, Germany has numerous campsites with varying levels of amenities and facilities. Camping is a popular choice, particularly in natural areas like the Black Forest or along the Baltic and North Sea coasts.

- Boutique Hotels: Germany boasts several boutique hotels that offer unique and stylish accommodations with a focus on design, art, and individuality. These hotels often provide a more personalized experience and can be found in major cities and cultural centers.

- Castle Hotels: For a truly memorable experience, Germany offers castle hotels where visitors can stay in historic castles and palaces. These accommodations combine history, elegance, and luxury, providing a unique glimpse into the past.

- *Hidden Gems* - Residential homes and apartments. Airbnb, Vrbo and Booking.com remain the best options for those wanting to try something along these lines. There really are some great options that can be found on these sites. Take a look! Some can genuinely be Hidden Gems.

Renown hotels

Most people tend to have a very distinct idea of what type of place they wish to stay in while traveling. As there are thousands of possible accommodations available in Germany, we can not list them all here. So, we thought it best to provide a list of ten rather distinctive options for visitors just to get a flavor:

- Adlon Kempinski (Berlin): This luxurious five-star hotel is located in Berlin and is known for its elegance and historic significance. Situated near the Brandenburg Gate, it offers beautifully appointed rooms, fine dining options, and impeccable service.

- Hotel Bayerischer Hof (Munich): Situated in the heart of Munich, the Hotel Bayerischer Hof is a renowned five-star hotel that blends traditional charm with modern amenities. It features stylish rooms, multiple restaurants and bars, a rooftop spa, and a theater.

- Hotel de Rome (Berlin): Housed in a historic building in Berlin, the Hotel de Rome offers a combination of classic elegance and contemporary design. Guests can enjoy spacious rooms, a rooftop terrace with stunning views, a spa, and a gourmet restaurant.

- Brenners Park-Hotel & Spa (Baden-Baden): Located in the scenic town of Baden-Baden, Brenners Park-Hotel & Spa is a luxury hotel set in a beautiful park. It offers elegant rooms, a world-class spa, Michelin-starred dining, and access to the nearby golf course.

- Roomers (Frankfurt): Situated in Frankfurt, Roomers is a stylish boutique hotel that exudes modern sophistication. Its chic rooms, trendy bar, and rooftop terrace make it a popular choice for visitors seeking a contemporary and vibrant atmosphere or for those just wanting to stop in for a bite or drink.

- Schloss Elmau Luxury Spa & Cultural Hideaway (Elmau): Nestled in the Bavarian Alps, Schloss Elmau is a luxury retreat offering a blend of nature, wellness, and cultural experiences. It features luxurious rooms, multiple spas, concert halls, gourmet restaurants, and a wide range of recreational activities.

- Breidenbacher Hof, a Capella Hotel (Düsseldorf): Situated in Düsseldorf, the Breidenbacher Hof is a prestigious five-star hotel known for its refined elegance and exceptional service. It offers luxurious rooms, a spa, fine dining options, and a prime location on the famous Königsallee shopping street.

- Hotel Vier Jahreszeiten Kempinski (Munich): Located in Munich, the Hotel Vier Jahreszeiten Kempinski is a grand five-star hotel with a rich history and opulent decor. It provides luxurious rooms, a rooftop pool, exquisite dining options, and a central location near the city's attractions.

- Schlosshotel Kronberg (Kronberg): Situated near Frankfurt, the Schlosshotel Kronberg is a castle hotel that combines historical charm with modern comforts. It offers elegant rooms, a golf course, a spa, and a tranquil setting amidst beautifully landscaped gardens.

- Ritz-Carlton, Berlin: The Ritz-Carlton is a prestigious five-star hotel in the heart of Berlin. It features elegant rooms, a luxury spa, fine dining options, and a central location near popular landmarks and shopping districts.

Chapter 6: Cultural Activities in Germany

Germany offers a rich cultural landscape with a wide range of activities that visitors can enjoy. Here are main cultural activities popular among tourists in Germany:

- Visit Museums: Germany is home to numerous world-class museums. Visitors can explore renowned institutions like the Museum Island in Berlin, which houses the Pergamon Museum and the Neues Museum, or the Museum Ludwig in Cologne, known for its modern and contemporary art collection.

- Explore Historical Sites: Germany is steeped in history, and visitors can immerse themselves in the country's past by visiting iconic sites such as the Brandenburg Gate in Berlin, Neuschwanstein Castle in Bavaria, and the Cologne Cathedral in Cologne.

- Attend Festivals: Germany is famous for its vibrant festivals. Oktoberfest in Munich is the world's largest beer festival, while the Christmas markets held throughout the country during the holiday season are a magical experience. Other notable festivals include Karneval in Cologne and the Berlin International Film Festival.

- Enjoy Classical Music: Germany has a rich classical music heritage, and attending a concert or opera performance is a popular cultural activity. Cities like Berlin, Munich, and Dresden are renowned for their world-class orchestras and opera houses.

- Experience the Berlin Wall: Visitors can explore the remnants of the Berlin Wall, which once divided the city. The East Side Gallery is a section of the wall that now serves as an open-air gallery, displaying vibrant murals by artists from around the world.

- Wander through Historic Old Towns: Germany's cities are filled with charming historic old towns. Visitors can stroll through cobblestone streets, admire medieval architecture, and soak in the unique atmosphere. Notable examples include Rothenburg ob der Tauber, Heidelberg, and Bamberg.

- Explore the Romantic Rhine Valley: The Rhine Valley offers picturesque landscapes dotted with vineyards, castles, and charming riverside towns. Taking a scenic boat cruise along the Rhine River or visiting iconic castles like Burg Eltz are popular cultural excursions.

- Visit Christmas Markets: During the holiday season, Germany's Christmas markets come alive with festive cheer. Visitors can browse through stalls selling crafts, enjoy traditional food and drinks, and soak up the enchanting atmosphere. The markets in Nuremberg, Dresden, and Cologne are particularly renowned, albeit are somewhat crowded.

- Experience Wagner's Operas at Bayreuth Festival: Classical music enthusiasts can immerse themselves in the works of Richard Wagner at the annual Bayreuth Festival. Held in Bayreuth, the festival showcases Wagner's operas in a legendary setting.

- Explore the Romantic Road: The Romantic Road is a scenic route that stretches through picturesque towns and landscapes, showcasing Germany's medieval and fairy-tale charm. Visitors can explore towns like Würzburg, Rothenburg ob der Tauber, and Füssen, which are close to Neuschwanstein Castle.

These cultural activities provide visitors with a glimpse into Germany's rich history, art, music, and traditions, allowing them to experience the country's unique cultural heritage firsthand.

Chapter 7: Nightlife And Festivals In Germany

Germany boasts a vibrant nightlife scene with diverse offerings in different parts of the country. Here's a glimpse into the nightlife experiences visitors can enjoy in various regions:

- Berlin: Berlin is renowned for its legendary nightlife, attracting partygoers worldwide. The city offers an eclectic mix of nightclubs, bars, and underground parties. Famous nightclubs like Berghain, Watergate, and Tresor are known for their electronic music scene. The district of Kreuzberg is popular for its alternative bars and live music venues.

- Hamburg: As Germany's second-largest city, Hamburg offers a lively nightlife scene. The St. Pauli district, particularly the Reeperbahn, is famous for its nightlife. It features a plethora of bars, clubs, and entertainment venues. Visitors can enjoy live music, theater shows, comedy performances, and vibrant nightlife along the bustling streets.

- Munich: Munich offers a mix of traditional beer halls and modern nightlife venues. The city is known for its beer gardens, where visitors can enjoy the unique Bavarian beer culture. The Glockenbachviertel neighborhood is popular for its trendy bars and clubs, while Maxvorstadt offers a vibrant student scene with bars and live music venues.

- Cologne: Cologne boasts a lively and inclusive nightlife. The Belgian Quarter and Ehrenfeld districts are known for their hip bars, clubs, and music venues. The city's LGBTQ+ scene is vibrant, with clubs like Bootshaus and Stadtgarten hosting energetic parties. Visitors can also enjoy the annual Cologne Carnival, a vibrant street festival known for its parades and festivities.

- Frankfurt: Frankfurt's nightlife caters to a diverse crowd, ranging from trendy clubs to upscale bars. The Bahnhofsviertel district is known for its nightlife offerings, with a mix of bars, clubs, and international cuisine. Sachsenhausen is popular for its traditional cider taverns, where visitors can savor regional specialties and enjoy a lively atmosphere.

- Leipzig: Leipzig has emerged as a vibrant cultural hub with a thriving nightlife scene. The city offers a mix of trendy bars, underground clubs, and alternative venues. The Karl-Liebknecht-Strasse, also known as the KarLi, is a popular street lined with bars and pubs. Visitors can also explore the vibrant live music scene, with Leipzig being a hub for indie, alternative, and electronic music.

- Düsseldorf: Düsseldorf offers a sophisticated and diverse nightlife experience. The Altstadt (Old Town) is famous for its "longest bar in the world," a stretch of bars, breweries, and pubs. Visitors can enjoy the city's vibrant beer culture and sample the local Altbier. The MedienHafen district is known for its upscale bars and trendy clubs, offering a more modern atmosphere.

- Stuttgart: Stuttgart offers a diverse range of nightlife options. The city is known for its vibrant club scene, with venues like Club Lehmann and Climax Institutes hosting renowned DJs and electronic music events. Visitors can also enjoy live music at venues like LKA Longhorn and Jazzclub Bix.

- Heidelberg: Heidelberg is not only famous for its historic charm but also offers a lively nightlife scene. The city's Old Town is dotted with cozy pubs, wine bars, and student-friendly establishments. Visitors can enjoy a relaxed evening sipping local wines or venture into the buzzing clubs and bars for a more energetic atmosphere.

- Nuremberg: Nuremberg's nightlife scene has a mix of trendy bars, pubs, and clubs. The city's historic center offers a range of establishments catering to different tastes. Visitors can explore the lively Kneipenquartier Gostenhof, known for its hip bars and live music venues, or enjoy cocktails in the elegant lounges of the Altstadt.

- Dresden: Dresden offers a unique blend of cultural attractions and a vibrant nightlife. The Neustadt district is known for its alternative scene, with a wide variety of pubs, bars, and clubs catering to various music genres. Visitors can enjoy live concerts, DJ sets, and themed parties in this lively part of the city.

- Bremen: Bremen's nightlife scene revolves around the Viertel district. This bohemian neighborhood is filled with lively bars, clubs, and music venues. Visitors can experience live music performances, indulge in craft beers, or stroll through the vibrant streets, soaking in the energetic atmosphere.

- Hannover: Hannover offers a diverse nightlife scene with something for everyone. The city's Raschplatz area is known for its vibrant clubs, hosting various music genres and dance parties. Visitors can also explore the historic Altstadt and enjoy cozy pubs, cocktail bars, and live music venues.

- Bonn: Bonn, the former capital of Germany, has a thriving nightlife centered around its student population. The city's nightlife hotspots can be found in the Altstadt and Poppelsdorf districts, where visitors can find a mix of bars, pubs, and clubs The Beethovenfest, an annual classical music festival, also attracts music enthusiasts from around the world.

Festivals

Germany hosts numerous vibrant festivals throughout the year, celebrating various aspects of its culture and traditions. Here are ten main festivals in Germany, along with the activities that visitors can enjoy:

1. Oktoberfest (Munich): One of the world's largest beer festivals, Oktoberfest takes place in Munich from late September to the first Sunday in October. Visitors can enjoy traditional Bavarian beer, indulge in delicious food like pretzels and sausages, and immerse themselves in the lively atmosphere of beer tents, parades, and carnival rides. Without a doubt, this is the most popular festival in Germany, and 2025 promises to have an expanded venue in several locations.

2. Christmas Markets (Various Cities): During the Advent season, Christmas markets pop up across Germany, enchanting visitors with their festive ambiance. Cities like Nuremberg, Cologne, Aachen and Munich are renowned for their Christmas markets. Visitors can browse stalls selling handmade crafts, enjoy warm mulled wine (Glühwein), savor traditional treats like gingerbread (Lebkuchen), and soak up the magical holiday spirit.

3. Cologne Carnival (Cologne): Cologne Carnival, known as the "fifth season," is a lively street festival held from November to February, with the main festivities taking place in February. Visitors can witness colorful parades, street parties, and costume balls. The highlight is Rose Monday (Rosenmontag), featuring

elaborate floats, music, and cheerful celebrations throughout the city. This carnival will go through February 13, 2025.

4. Berlin International Film Festival (Berlinale) (Berlin): The Berlin International Film Festival, held annually in February, attracts cinephiles and industry professionals from around the world. Visitors can attend film screenings, premieres, and special events, and explore the diverse range of films showcased at different venues across Berlin. The schedule is through February 16 in 2025 and roughly a few days later in 2026.

5. Beethovenfest (Bonn): The Beethovenfest is a renowned classical music festival held in Bonn, the birthplace of Ludwig van Beethoven. Taking place in September and October, the festival features concerts by renowned orchestras, chamber music performances, and special Beethoven-themed events, celebrating the composer's legacy.

6. Wagner Festival (Bayreuth): The Wagner Festival, held in Bayreuth, pays homage to the works of composer Richard Wagner. It takes place from late July to August and features performances of Wagner's operas in the iconic Festspielhaus. Visitors can immerse themselves in the world of Wagnerian music and witness the grandeur of these legendary productions.

7. Carnival of Cultures (Berlin): The Carnival of Cultures is a multicultural street festival held in Berlin in May or June. Visitors can experience a vibrant celebration of diversity through music, dance performances, street food, and arts and

crafts. The highlight is the colorful carnival parade, showcasing the city's multiculturalism and promoting cultural exchange.

8. Hamburger Dom (Hamburg): Hamburger Dom is a large fair held three times a year in Hamburg. Visitors can enjoy thrilling rides, indulge in carnival food, and play games at the numerous stalls. The festival also features live music, fireworks, and other entertainment, creating a fun-filled atmosphere for families and friends.

9. Karneval der Kulturen (Carnival of Cultures) (Berlin): Karneval der Kulturen is a multicultural street festival in Berlin, celebrating the city's diversity. Held in May or June, the festival showcases music, dance performances, culinary delights, and arts and crafts from various cultures. Visitors can join the vibrant parade, participate in workshops, and enjoy live music stages featuring international artists.

10. Cannstatter Volksfest (Stuttgart): Cannstatter Volksfest, also known as the Stuttgart Beer Festival, is the second-largest beer festival in Germany, after Oktoberfest. Held from late September to early October, visitors can enjoy beer tents, traditional food, fairground rides, and live music. The festival also includes a colorful parade and fireworks.

These festivals offer visitors an opportunity to immerse themselves in German culture, traditions, and celebrations. From beer festivals to music events and street carnivals to Christmas markets, these vibrant festivals showcase the country's rich heritage and create memorable experiences for all who attend.

We would strongly suggest that you do look in advance for the dates these are being held as there may be a little variance year to year, and some events at these carnivals may well require advance booking or possibly reservations day of.

Chapter 8: Souvenirs And Shopping in Germany

Germany is known for its diverse and vibrant shopping scene, offering a wide range of options for visitors. Here are some popular shopping places in Germany:

1. Kurfürstendamm (Ku'damm) - Berlin: Kurfürstendamm, often referred to as Ku'damm, is Berlin's most famous shopping street. It is home to high-end boutiques, department stores like KaDeWe, luxury brands, and designer shops. Visitors can also find popular international brands, local fashion stores, and specialty shops.

2. Zeil - Frankfurt: Zeil is Frankfurt's premier shopping street, lined with a mix of high-end boutiques, department stores, and popular retail chains. Visitors can explore the Zeilgalerie shopping mall and nearby shopping centers like MyZeil, where they can find a variety of fashion, accessories, electronics, and more.

3. Mönckebergstraße - Hamburg: Mönckebergstraße is Hamburg's main shopping street, offering a wide range of shops and department stores. Visitors can find international fashion brands, well-known retail chains, and specialty stores. The street is also home to the historic Alsterhaus department store.

4. Maximilianstraße - Munich: Maximilianstraße is Munich's prestigious shopping boulevard, known for its luxury boutiques, designer stores, and upscale brands. Visitors can browse

through high-end fashion, jewelry, watches, and exclusive accessories. The street also showcases beautiful architecture and is a pleasant place for a stroll.

5. Düsseldorf-Königsallee (Kö): Düsseldorf's Königsallee, known as Kö, is a renowned luxury shopping destination. It features elegant fashion boutiques, upscale department stores like Breuninger and Kö-Galerie, and flagship stores of international luxury brands. The street is famous for its wide canal and beautiful tree-lined promenade.

6. Schildergasse - Cologne: Schildergasse is Cologne's main shopping street, bustling with shops, department stores, and fashion retailers. Visitors can find a mix of well-known brands, local boutiques, and specialty stores. The street also offers cafes, restaurants, and street performers, creating a lively shopping atmosphere.

7. Kaufingerstraße - Munich: Kaufingerstraße is one of Munich's busiest shopping streets, located in the city center. It is a pedestrian-friendly street with a range of shops, including fashion retailers, accessory stores, souvenir shops, and more. The street leads to the famous Marienplatz, where visitors can explore additional shops and the popular Viktualienmarkt.

8. Hohe Straße and Schildergasse - Cologne: Hohe Straße and Schildergasse form a popular shopping district in Cologne's city center. These streets offer a mix of international fashion brands, department stores, and specialty shops. Visitors can also find

local boutiques, jewelry stores, and perfumeries. The district is known for its vibrant atmosphere and lively street life.

9. Schwabing - Munich: Schwabing is a trendy neighborhood in Munich, known for its bohemian vibe and unique shops. Visitors can explore independent boutiques, vintage stores, art galleries, and concept stores. The area also offers stylish cafes, bars, and restaurants, making it a popular spot for shopping and leisure.

10. Rothenburg ob der Tauber - Bavaria: Rothenburg ob der Tauber, a charming medieval town in Bavaria, is famous for its picturesque streets and unique shops. Visitors can wander through the town's narrow alleys and find shops selling traditional German crafts, Christmas decorations, souvenirs, and more. The town's traditional German Christmas stores are particularly popular.

Souvenirs

Germany offers a wide variety of souvenirs that showcase its rich culture, craftsmanship, and traditions. Here are ten main souvenirs that visitors can consider, along with suggested places to buy them:

1. Beer Steins (Bierkrüge): Beer steins are traditional German mugs made of ceramic or glass, often adorned with intricate designs and lid toppers. Visitors can find beer steins in souvenir shops, gift stores, and specialty beer shops throughout Germany.

2. Christmas Ornaments (Weihnachtsschmuck): Germany is renowned for its beautiful Christmas ornaments. Handcrafted glass ornaments, wooden nutcrackers, and pyramids are popular choices. Visitors can find them in Christmas markets, specialty shops, and souvenir stores, with Nuremberg and Dresden being famous for their Christmas markets.

3. Cuckoo Clocks (Kuckucksuhren): Cuckoo clocks are iconic symbols of Germany's Black Forest region. These intricately carved wooden clocks with a charming cuckoo bird that announces the time are widely available in souvenir shops and clock stores in the Black Forest area.

4. Traditional Clothing (Trachten): Traditional German clothing, such as dirndls (for women) and lederhosen (for men), make unique souvenirs. Visitors can find them in specialty clothing stores, tourist shops, and markets, especially in Bavaria, during festivals like Oktoberfest.

5. Nutella: Although not a traditional German product, Germany has a special connection to Nutella. The world's largest Nutella factory is located in the town of Stadtallendorf. Visitors can purchase Nutella jars or Nutella-themed merchandise in supermarkets, local shops, and the Nutella factory store.

6. Black Forest Ham (Schwarzwälder Schinken): Black Forest ham is a famous German delicacy known for its rich flavor. Visitors can buy vacuum-sealed packages of Black Forest ham in gourmet food stores, butcher shops, and local markets, particularly in the Black Forest region.

7. Berlin Ampelmännchen: The Ampelmännchen, the iconic pedestrian traffic signal figures from East Germany, have become a beloved symbol of Berlin. Visitors can find Ampelmännchen-themed souvenirs, including keychains, magnets, and clothing, in souvenir shops throughout Berlin.

8. German Beer (Bier): Germany is renowned for its beer culture, and visitors can bring home a taste of German brewing traditions. Local breweries, beer specialty shops, and supermarkets offer a wide range of German beers and beer gift sets.

9. Haribo Gummy Bears: Haribo, the famous German confectionery brand, originated in Germany. Haribo gummy bears are beloved worldwide. Visitors can purchase Haribo gummy bears and other Haribo candies in supermarkets, candy shops, and souvenir stores across Germany.

10. Ritter Sport Chocolate: Ritter Sport is a popular German chocolate brand known for its square-shaped bars and a wide variety of flavors. Visitors can find Ritter Sport chocolates in supermarkets, convenience stores, and dedicated chocolate shops throughout Germany.

These souvenirs capture the essence of German culture, culinary delights, and traditional crafts. Visitors can find them in various cities and regions, ranging from specialized shops to local markets, ensuring they have a piece of Germany to take home as a lasting memory.

Chapter 9: Tips For Traveling in Germany

- Learn basic German phrases: While many Germans speak English, it's always helpful to know a few basic German phrases. Learning greetings, saying "please" (bitte) and "thank you" (danke), and understanding simple directions can enhance your interactions and show respect for the local culture.

- Carry cash: While credit cards are widely accepted in major establishments, it's still a good idea to carry some cash, especially when visiting smaller shops, local markets, or rural areas where cash might be the preferred payment method.

- Respect quiet hours: Germany has strict noise regulations, particularly during "quiet hours" (Ruhezeit) in the evenings and on Sundays. Avoid making loud noises, playing music at high volumes, or engaging in disruptive activities during these times to show consideration for others.

- Observe recycling practices: Germany is known for its commitment to recycling. Be mindful of separating your waste into appropriate bins for paper, plastics, glass, and organic waste. Look for color-coded bins and follow the recycling guidelines to contribute to Germany's eco-friendly practices which most strictly adhere to.

- Be punctual: Germans value punctuality, so it's important to be on time for appointments, meetings, and reservations. Arriving a few minutes early is considered polite. If you're running late, be sure to inform the person you're meeting.

- Follow public transportation etiquette: When using public transportation, such as buses, trams, and trains, adhere to the established etiquette. Offer your seat to elderly or pregnant passengers, keep noise levels to a minimum, and validate your ticket before boarding if required.

- Respect personal space: Germans value their personal space, so it's essential to respect this cultural norm. It is a good practice to always maintain an appropriate distance when interacting with others and avoid touching or hugging people you've just met unless it's customary in the specific context.

- Be mindful of Sundays: Sundays in Germany are generally quiet and observed as a day of rest. Many shops, including supermarkets, are closed on Sundays, and there are restrictions on noise and certain activities. Plan accordingly and use Sundays to explore parks, museums, or enjoy leisurely walks. A number of options are usually available.

- Follow dining etiquette: When dining in Germany, it's customary to wait for everyone to be served before starting to eat. Additionally, remember to say "Guten Appetit" (enjoy your meal) before you begin eating. It's also common to place your knife and fork parallel on your plate when finished to signal that you're done.

- Explore beyond the big cities: While cities like Berlin, Munich, and Hamburg are popular destinations, don't miss the opportunity to explore the smaller towns and rural areas. Germany has stunning countryside, charming villages, and historic sites that offer a different perspective on the country's culture and history.

Germany Travel Guide 2023

IMPORTANT TO NOTE for 2025 !!

Please be aware that around May 2025 (Expected), a visa will be required for travelers with United States or Canadian passports. A special travel authorization—ETIAS, which stands for the European Travel Information and Authorization System—will be required for those travelers. The cost is expected to be less than US $10, and the process is simple, requiring online registration, and should be good for three years. Registration will be required for Germany, and 29 other European countries.

Conclusion

Putting together a Germany tour book is difficult. There is so much to see and do in this highly diverse country that one would really need months to take it all in. In these pages, we have attempted to provide you, the traveler, an overview of what Germany has to offer, some helpful tips, places to see, some hidden gem type of locations, and more. We believe this can help you establish what it is you want to see on your trip and "guide" you in the right direction.

Germany offers travelers a wide choice of experiences, combining a fascinating culture, a long history, breathtaking scenery, and kind people. It offers something for every kind of visitor, whether you want to take in the beauty of the Black Forest or the romantic Rhine Valley or explore bustling cities like Berlin and Munich.

Visitors can savor mouthwatering cuisine, try renowned brews, and participate in customary events. While the nation's commitment to sustainability and recycling provides an example of environmental concern, its well-connected transportation system makes it simple to move around and explore different places.

When traveling to Germany, it's crucial to respect quiet hours, observe local customs and etiquette, and learn a few basic German phrases to improve your communication. Germany guarantees a wonderful trip, whether exploring historical sites, looking for one-of-a-kind souvenirs, trying out that incredible German cuisine, or just taking in the country's breathtaking natural beauty.

So prepare to accept new experiences, pack your bags, and set out on a journey that will show you Germany's heart and soul.